Hinde Bergner

On Long Winter Nights…

This publication has been made possible by the generous support of
the Ravitch Book Fund
of the Jewish Public Library, Montreal, Canada

Harvard University
Center for Jewish Studies

Hinde Bergner

On Long Winter Nights…
Memoirs of a Jewish Family
in a Galician Township (1870–1900)

Translated from the Yiddish, edited,
and with an introduction
by
Justin Daniel Cammy

Distributed by
Harvard University Press
Cambridge, Massachusetts and London, England
2005

Library of Congress Cataloging-in-Publication Data

Bergner, Hinde, 1870–1942.
   [In di lange vinternekht. English]
   On long winter nights— : memoirs of a Jewish family in a Galician township (1870–1900) / Hinde Bergner ; translated from the Yiddish, edited, and with an introduction by Justin Daniel Cammy.
     p. cm.
   Includes bibliographical references.
   ISBN 0-674-01969-5 (cloth) — ISBN 0-674-01970-9 (paper)
   1. Bergner, Hinde, 1870–1942. 2. Jews—Poland—Radymno—Biography. 3. Jews—Poland—Radymno—Social life and customs—19th century. 4. Radymno (Poland)—Social life and customs—19th century. I. Cammy, Justin Daniel. II. Title.

DS135.P63B41413 2005

2005046372

Cover design by Duy-Khuong Van.

Cover art and inside sketches by Yosl Bergner.

Book production and design by CDL Press, POB 34454, Bethesda, MD 20827.

Publisher: Harvard University Center for Jewish Studies.

Contents

Hinde Bergner, Yerslev 1888

Note on Translation and Acknowledgments

This translation from the Yiddish is based on Hinde Bergner's *In di lange vinternekht...: mishpokhe-zikhroynes fun a shtetl in galitsye (1870–1900)*, posthumously published in Montreal in 1946 by her sons, the Yiddish writers Melekh Ravitsh and Herts Bergner.

The transliteration of Yiddish and Hebrew terms always presents particular challenges. With an eye to retaining the cultural allusions of the original, I chose to transliterate rather than translate a number of terms unique to Jewish tradition. These terms are explained in a glossary at the end of the memoir. In transliterating these terms and names in the text of the memoir, I generally followed the standard system of phonetic Yiddish transliteration accepted by the YIVO. In so doing, I acknowledge that this system does not take into accounts variants in Yiddish pronunciation, especially the way Hinde Bergner's Galician Yiddish would have sounded. I decided to maintain consistency by transliterating most Hebrew constituent elements of Yiddish according to this system. For instance, the memoir speaks of *Khanike, khosid,* and *Shvues* rather than their more common appearances in English transliteration as Hanukah, Hasid, and Shavuot.

Place names are among the most difficult challenges for any translator of works from Eastern Europe. With political upheavals and shifting borders, the names of cities and towns often changed spelling or pronunciation to reflect new political realities. The memoir retains the Yiddish place names used by Hinde Bergner since they constituted a natural part of her Eastern European Jewish homeland. For alternate spellings in Polish, Ukrainian, and German, see Gary Mokotoff and Sallyann Amdur Sack, *Where We Once Walked: A Guide to Jewish Communties Destroyed in the Holocaust.*

My heartfelt appreciation to Yosl Bergner, Hinde Bergner's grandson, for his enthusiastic permission to proceed with the translation of his grandmother's memoirs and his persistent encouragement. His wife, Audrey Bergner, read through an entire early draft of the manuscript with great sensitivity, suggesting several improvements. Yosl welcomed my wife and me into his studio in Tel Aviv on several occasions, dazzling us with his stories of the many Yiddish and Hebrew literary and cultural figures he has met and worked with over the years. He also drew to my attention several unpublished manuscript pages excised from the original Yiddish edition, which are published here for the first time. I am delighted that his drawings accompany this English edition of his grandmother's memoirs.

My special thanks to Ruth R. Wisse, Len Wisse, Rachel Rubinstein, and Ernest Benz for reading the manuscript prior to publication. Thanks also to Professors Wisse and Jay Harris for guiding the translation through to publication under the auspices of the Center for Jewish Studies at Harvard University. Financial support for the translation came in the form of a grant from the Melekh Ravitsh Book Fund of the Jewish Public Library of Montreal, Canada. I was delighted to discover that Hinde Bergner's son—Melekh Ravitsh—singles out Professor Wisse's parents in the acknowledgments to his own memoirs for their help in bringing his work to press. I hope that she finds some satisfaction in the fact that, several generations later, a student of hers now helps bring the memoirs of Ravitsh's mother to an English readership.

Justin Cammy
Smith College

Preface

Hinde Bergner's memoir of family life in Galicia in the last years of the nineteenth century is the recollections of an older woman who turned to writing to soothe her loneliness. Composed in the late 1930s, a time of great anxiety for Polish Jewry, when her sons were already successful Yiddish writers living abroad, the memoir was intended to provide her children with a sense of their immediate ancestors and serve as a bridge between generations. Perhaps because of the intimate nature of her imagined audience, it is written in a lively, irreverent tone. Her anecdotes about her many teachers and matchmakers, the simple faith and petty foibles of her extended family, domestic religion and female spirituality, her private ambitions, and the everyday tensions between traditional Jewish society and the attractiveness of modern European culture make the memoir valuable to readers interested in gaining a first-hand, woman's perspective on life in one Galician Jewish town in a time of rapid cultural transformation.[1]

I might have been content to leave Hinde Bergner's memoir in its original Yiddish if not for my experiences as a teaching fellow a decade ago in a course entitled "Jewish life in Eastern Europe" offered by Professor Jay Harris at Harvard. Many undergraduates enrolled in the course to satisfy Harvard's requirement for study of a foreign culture. For many it was their first and only critical introduction to Jews in any context. Students were guided through the most significant religious and secular movements in Jewish Eastern Europe between 1750 and

---

1. For a list of twenty-one memoirs by Eastern European women born between 1865–1900, see Paula Hyman, *Gender and Assimilation in Modern Jewish History* (Seattle: University of Washington Press, 1995), 64–65. Recently, several memoirs from that list have been translated into English, including those of Pauline Wengeroff, *Rememberings: The World of a Russian Jewish Woman in the 19th Century* (Bethesda, Md.:University Press of Maryland, 2000) and Puah Rokovsky, *My Life as a Radical Jewish Woman: Memoirs of a Zionist Feminist in Poland* (Bloomington, Ind.: Indiana University Press, 2001).

1914, from the emergence of the religious revivalist movement known as Hasidism and its traditionalist opponent, Misnagdism, through the development of the *Haskole* (the Jewish Enlightenment), the birth of such modern political and cultural movements as the socialist Bund, Zionism, Yiddishism, and the rise of modern Yiddish and Hebrew literatures. The course approached its subject through the prism of intellectual, rather than social history, and wanted students to come to an understanding of the major religious and cultural transformations in Jewish Eastern Europe through a reading of primary sources. Translation obviously posed the most significant obstacle to the development of a representative reading list, since almost all primary materials were in Hebrew, Yiddish, or one of the co-territorial European languages. Religious high culture was almost exclusively the dominion of men, which explains why women did not figure as authors of Hasidic and Misnagdic texts. Even when Jewish society opened up under the combined influences of the *Haskole* and modernization, the gender gap among secular Jewish writers and thinkers took several generations to narrow. The sphere of domestic (or popular) religion was somewhat more fruitful, in that students were introduced to the one area of religious life where women had historically played a role in the creation of spiritual texts known as *tkhines,* Yiddish supplicatory prayers recited privately by women when fulfilling their religious obligations.[2]

To be sure, the course did devote significant attention to the experiences of Jewish women in so far as they might inform our understanding of important intellectual, religious, cultural and literary developments. For instance, a Hebrew ethical will by the Gaon of Vilna (Elijah ben Solomon Zalman, 1720–1797), one of the giant Torah scholars of the Eastern European Jewish experience, provided important insights into the way a master of Talmud thought about the moral education of his children and envisioned a model family structure for Jews. The Gaon's specific instructions to his wife regarding how his daughters ought to be educated (which included their rigorous study of moral literature in Yiddish and the command to refrain from all frivolous talk so as to avoid even accidental slander) refined the way students understood the division of gender roles within the most pious traditional households. Later in the course, students read a segment

2. See Chava Weissler, *Voices of the Matriarchs: Listening to the Prayers of Early Modern Jewish Women* (Boston: Beacon Press, 1998).

from Barukh Epstein's (1860–1942) *Meqor Barukh* in which the author writes about several conversations he had with his aunt, Rayne Batye Berlin. Rayne was the wife of Naftali Zvi Yehudah Berlin (known as Ha-Neziv from his initials), who was the head of the *yeshive* at Voloz-hin, one of the most prestigious Talmud academies in tsarist Russia. As the granddaughter of Khayim of Volozhin (disciple of the Gaon of Vilna), who founded the *yeshive* and ran it from 1803 to 1821, and the daughter of Yitskhok of Volozhin, who headed the *yeshive* from 1821 to 1849, she (and not her husband) would likely have been the next head of the Volozhin academy had she been a man. Her nephew's memoirs underscored the deep frustrations of this talented woman, whose own aspirations for intellectual respect in the world of Torah scholarship were stymied by the fact that women could never play a for-mal role in communal leadership or scholarship. The text revealed Rayne's intimate familiarity with Jewish religious texts. What surprised students most was that despite her frustration, Rayne ultimately swal-lowed her own scholarly ambitions and pride. By focusing her energies on the support of her husband in his endeavors, she managed to see herself as a valued contributor to the holy work of Torah study. Still later, Yehuda Leyb Gordon's (1830–1892) famous poem, "*Kotso shel yud*" (The Tip of the Yud), exposed students to one of the sharpest cri-tiques of traditional Jewish marriage by an exponent of the Russian *Haskole*. Its bitter satire of rabbinic legalism suggested that rabbis were more interested in showing off their own intellectual prowess by pars-ing the fine points of Jewish law (known as *pilpul*) than concerned with how it might affect the lives of ordinary Jews. Gordon's Hebrew classic drew attention to the precarious position of women who were at the mercy of their husbands (and the approval of rabbinic courts) to pro-vide them with a bill of divorce. The poem casts a rabbi as its villain by having him void a bill of divorce when he finds fault with a single letter in a signature. This renders the heroine an *agune* (literally "chained"), a woman who cannot remarry because she is not legally divorced.

The German memoirs of Pauline Wengeroff (1833–1916), born into a Misnagdic family and married to a Hasidic man, offered a cri-tique of a different sort. For one, her memoir was the only text in the course in which a woman's voice was presented unfiltered by men. Wengeroff's memoir highlighted the recklessness with which many Jews, especially Jewish men, cast off the traditions of earlier genera-tions for the promise of personal fulfillment through assimilation. She recalls the fears of her mother, who confided: "Two things I know for certain: I and my generation will certainly live and die as Jews. Our grandchildren will not live and die as Jews. I just don't know what will become of my children." Her memoirs ask a basic question: why was it that most Jews could not find a balance between their own traditions and modernity, choosing instead to jettison almost everything that had been dear to their ancestors for generations for the hope of fitting into Europe? Students presumed that Jewish women had much to gain from the dissolution of traditional society, and it was refreshing to see them grapple with a text that mourned the destruction of the traditional way of life in which its author had grown up. Wengeroff describes her husband coming home one day and ordering her to stop covering her hair (as was custom for observant married women); soon after, he banished kosher meat from the home. "All these men and their modern values," she laments, "they reserve for themselves the right to seek political and economic advancement. But when they came home they were petty tyrants." Wengeroff underlines a central paradox in the way embourgeoisement was experienced by Jewish men and women. While her husband chose to divest himself of all Jewish practices and symbols as part of a process of personal liberation, his freedoms did not extend to greater autonomy for his wife but rather threatened her freedom to retain Jewish customs.

Though the condition, frustrations, and hopes of Jewish women appeared regularly throughout the course, several students remained thirsty not just for more sessions *about* women, but for more women's voices. In the absence of such materials, some students projected onto the earlier period their own, often contentious, ideas about "patriarchal society." Initially then, my translation of Hinde Bergner's memoirs began as an attempt to fill a pressing bibliographic need by providing students of Jewish Eastern Europe with a short, readable text that reveals the constant—and highly individualized—negotiation between tradition and secular enticements.

Hinde Bergner was born on 11 October 1870 in Redim (Polish Radymno), a *shtetl* or Jewish market town in Galicia on the shores of the river Rada. Redim was sandwiched between the small cities of Pshemish (Przemysl) and Yerslev (Yereslev, Jaroslaw).[3] While she was growing up, Jews constituted almost half of Redim's population. Hinde lived her entire life in eastern Galicia until the outbreak of the Second World War. Galicia was one of the historic regions of Poland that can no longer be found on maps.[4] Its territory of some 80,000 square kilometers north of the Carpathian mountains today spans portions of southeastern Poland and northwestern Ukraine.

Between 1772 and 1919 Galicia was a province of the Austro-Hungarian Empire, annexed to the Hapsburg lands during the first partition of the Polish-Lithuanian Commonwealth in 1772.[5] It was an ethnically diverse region. It boasted the largest proportion of Jews of any region in east-central Europe outside the kingdom of Poland. Galicia's Jews (known by some as *Galitsianer*) lived amidst two larger national groups, the Poles and the Ukrainians. The Poles constituted

3. According to the census of 1880, there were 898 Jews in Redim when Hinde was a young girl, 47% of its total population. On the eve of World War I, the town's Jewish population peaked at 1,300, falling again to 808 Jews by 1921. By comparison, in 1890 there were 10,998 Jews in Pshemish. Their numbers grew to 16,062 (30% of the city's population) in 1910, and to 18,360 (38%) by 1921. In 1890 Yerslev's Jewish population was 4,820 out of a total of 18,065 (27%).

4. In Jewish historiography Galicia generally has been considered a chapter of Polish-Jewish history. As a result there are no general histories of Galician Jewry. Recently, a special issue of *Polin*, "Galicia: Jews, Poles, and Ukrainians, 1772–1918," filled this scholarly lacuna. See Israel Bartal and Antony Polonsky, *Polin: Studies in Polish Jewry* 12 (The Littman Library of Jewish Civilization, 1999). See also J. Schoenfeld, *Shtetl Memoirs: Jewish Life in Galicia under the Austro-Hungarian Empire and in the Reborn Poland, 1898–1939* (Hoboken, N.J.: Ktav, 1985); Nathan Michael Gelber, "Galicia," *Encyclopaedia Judaica*, v. 16 (New York and Jerusalem: The Macmillan Company and Keter Publishing House, 1971), 1325–1332. The best general history of Galicia is Paul Robert Magocsi, *Galicia: A Historical Survey and Bibliographic Guide* (Toronto: University of Toronto Press, 1983).

5. After World War I, Galicia was formally included in the reconstituted Polish republic. In 1939, western Galicia was conquered by the Nazis, while its eastern half fell under the control of the Soviet Union. In 1941, Nazi Germany took control of eastern Galicia as well, murdering most of Galicia's Jews. After the war, Galicia was once again divided, this time between Poland and Soviet Ukraine.

much of the landed gentry, and it was the dominant Polish culture that proved most attractive to the emerging intelligentsia and bourgeoisie looking to acculturate into Europe. Jewish life in Galicia expanded considerably during the period of Austrian rule. Jews grew in number from 144,200 in 1776 to 871,985 in 1910. In 1869, a year before Hinde's birth, there was a total population of 5,450,000 in Galicia. The Poles numbered 2,510,000 and the Ukrainians 2,316,000. The region's 575,000 Jews were the balance at more than 10% of the total population. By 1890, when Hinde was a grown woman, Jews constituted 770,500 of 6,600,000 inhabitants of Galicia, or 11.7%. Three quarters of the region's Jews lived in the small cities and towns of eastern Galicia, where they constituted a much larger percentage of the local population. In dozens of Jewish market towns like Hinde's Redim, Jews amounted to half of the population. Though extreme poverty and political anxiety led to the emigration of 172,500 Jews from eastern Galicia between 1881 and 1910 (most to the United States), the Jewish population of Galicia continued to expand until the eve of World War I. By this time, the majority (53%) of Galician Jewry engaged in some form of commerce, 25% in industry and crafts, 11% in the liberal professions such as medicine, law, or civil service, and 11% in agriculture.[6]

Throughout much of the nineteenth century Hinde Bergner's *shtetl* of Redim was dominated by the followers of the Hasidic master Tsvi Elimelekh Dynow (1785–1841), and the Belz Hasidic dynasty. Hasidism was the dominant form of religious affiliation in Galicia from the 1830s. Beyond Hasidism, however, the memoir helps us to see the degree to which folk religion and more domestic forms of personal women's piety helped inform the spirituality of the community. Though women were excluded from communal leadership and were not counted in prayer quorums, Hinde shows that their religiosity was, in many cases, just as refined as that of their fathers, husbands, and sons. Hinde's portraits of her mother's pious preparations for the Sabbath and her selfless charity offer a positive model of traditional life, even if Hinde ultimately chose a different path.

6. Magocsi, 229.

Life in small Galician *shtetlekh* like Redim was modest. Most Jews barely eked out a living in petty trade or in providing services to the townsfolk and peasantry. However, a small minority was economically more established. Among this class were those who historically had been charged by Polish gentry with the management of their estates. Others were provided with licenses and even monopolies over such important industries as brewing, milling, forestry, and tax collection.[7] Hinde's own family was fortunate to manage an estate for a time, providing her with a comparatively comfortable childhood.

The nineteenth century was marked by significant cultural upheaval and competition within Eastern European Jewry. The spread of Hasidism was challenged early on by the Jewish Enlightenment or *Haskole*, whose reformers were known as *maskilim*. Early leaders of the *Haskole* in Galicia included Naftali Herts Homberg (1749–1841), charged by the authorities with setting up modern, secular Jewish schools at the beginning of the nineteenth century, and Josef Perl (1777–1839), author of one of the most devastating literary satires of Hasidism, *Megale temirin* (Revealer of Secrets, 1819). In Galicia the *Haskole* gained a foothold in large cities such as Cracow and Lemberg, and filtered down through medium-size communities such as Brody and Tarnopol to smaller towns. By the latter half of the nineteenth century, the critiques of tradition by the *Haskole* and the pressures of modernization led to the rise of assimilationist circles, though even the assimilationists were torn between German or Polish culture. Later, Jewish youth was drawn to local forms of Zionism and Jewish socialism. These shifts had a particular impact in the area of education. While most Jews still chose to send their children to the traditional Jewish *kheyder* (primary school), by 1890 Jews constituted 18% of students in Galician *gymnasia* (secondary schools), with the percentages of Jewish girls attending these secular institutions even higher.[8] More than 20% of students at the University of Lemberg in 1897 were Jews. Though these intercultural contacts were naturally higher in Galicia's major centers than in provincial towns, the numbers nevertheless point to

7. Jozef Buszko, "The Consequences of Galician Autonomy after 1867" in Bartal and Polonsky, *Polin* 12 (1999), 124–125.

8. For more on the education of boys and girls in this period, see Shaul Stampfer, "Gender Differentiation and Education of Jewish Women in Nineteenth-Century Eastern Europe," *Polin* 7 (1992): 63–87.

increasing Jewish acculturation. Like many other families of economic means, Hinde's family struggled to satisfy her determination to acquire a more worldly education while attempting to instill in her a respect for tradition.

The central element of Hinde's self-representation borrows from pre-existing tropes of maskilic literature. Yiddish and Hebrew literature of the Jewish enlightenment is defined by its satiric orientation toward traditional society. Its stock themes point to the deficiencies and foolishness of the rabbinate, the inadequacies of Jewish education, and the corrosive effects of early marriage—precisely the material that is the focus of Hinde's memoir. Her mockery of her *kheyder* teachers, her matchmakers, and even the Hasidic *rebbe* her father frequents for blessings shows that women were just as invested in the struggle for self-emancipation as were men, and in many cases were more European in their perspective owing to the fact that their traditional education was not as rigorous as that provided to boys. Yet Hinde's frustration with the traditional world is a gradual process rather than a sudden break. Though as a young woman she seems constantly to challenge her parents' expectations of her, especially in the areas of education, dress, career, and marriage, her sympathetic portraits of those family members who are able to maintain a traditional life betray a certain admiration and tenderness for that level of commitment. At the same time, Hinde is unforgiving in matters of religious hypocrisy. She recounts how one of her teachers made certain to hit his female students on their clothes, never on bare skin, so as not to transgress certain laws of sexual modesty. She mocks Hasidic *rebbes* who demand advance payment to intercede with God on behalf of their followers, or those individuals who are outwardly observant but hide behind drawn blinds to eat on fast days. Lest readers think that domestic violence was not part of *shtetl* life, she describes how her sister-in-law physically abused and humiliated her brother.

By the late nineteenth century, young Galician Jews were increasingly under the influence of non-Jewish European society. Hinde read fluently in three languages—Yiddish, Polish, and German. This multilingualism was a natural part of Jewish life in Eastern Europe, and Hinde's memoirs reveal just how much cross-cultural fertilization was occurring, even in the provinces. She spoke to her family's Gentile servants in Polish, she was sophisticated enough to enjoy both Yiddish and Polish theater, and she even wrote love letters in Polish to her brother's fiancée on his behalf. Her attempts to learn French and play the piano show how the tastes of the Polish nobility influenced well-off Jewish families. Some of her more Europeanized teachers introduced her to German and Polish literature, and she was aware of people her age elsewhere reading Schiller. Her exposure to European culture through books was symptomatic of an entire generation of young "reading Jewish women" who were instrumental in importing modern ideas and sensibilities into traditional society, and distanced themselves from texts such as the *Korbn-minkhe* and *Tsena-urene* that had long constituted the traditional library of Ashkenazic women.[9] Hinde's desire for romantic love and secular education, her interest in theater, music, literature, and other languages, and her refusal to shear her hair after marriage and wear the traditional Jewish wig, or *shaytl*, are markers of bourgeois ambition and individuality. The confused and sometimes desperate reaction of Hinde's parents, especially her mother, to her behavior and desires makes the generation gap palpable. The desire on the part of young Jews to participate in general society was not without its dangers, however, as we see in the episode involving her brother and the military draft. Jewish antipathy toward military service reflected the ambivalent position of Jews as political outsiders ordered to serve an authority that was, at best, lukewarm about their place in European society.

During Hinde's childhood, her father managed an estate and ran a granary, where she also worked. He relied on her to help him run his business. At the beginning of the memoir, we see a tension between Hinde and her father precisely because she wants to devote herself to her education while he has been counting on her to take over his accounting. The incident reflects the degree to which women were expected to contribute to the economic management of the household. As Paula Hyman has suggested, the "strong capable working woman was the dominant cultural ideal, in contrast to the ideal of woman as the creator of a domestic haven (or heaven) that prevailed in the bourgeois West."[10] It was from this ideal and the shadow of early marriage that Hinde was attempting to free herself through education.

---

9. See Iris Parush, *Reading Jewish Women: Marginality and Modernization in Nineteenth-Century Eastern European Jewish Society* (Waltham: Brandeis University Press, 2004).

10. Hyman, *Gender and Assimilation*, 68. Hyman provides a list of other texts that focus on the place of Jewish women in the local economy, 67–68.

Since the Jewish family was the basic social unit for the transmission of traditional culture, the arrangement of an appropriate match was of supreme concern to Jewish parents. In the middle and upper classes, several factors determined the most desirable unions, including *yikhes* (family lineage), wealth, the level of Torah scholarship of the potential groom, and a consideration of a woman's ability to run an efficient household. Hinde's family turned for assistance to *shad-khonim*, professional Jewish matchmakers who were expected to keep all these considerations in mind and act as intermediaries between families. The incompetent, threatening *shadkhn* is a common motif of maskilic literature, since he represented the power of parents to thwart modernity's promise of individual self-fulfillment.[11] Since children were engaged and married before they could economically and psychologically fend for themselves, many families supported the young couple in the initial years of marriage through the custom of *kest*, which involved the young couple boarding at the home of the bride's parents. Even Hinde, whose marriage at the age of twenty was considered very late for the times,[12] lived initially with her husband Efrayim in Redim off her parents' *kest* and the funds from the marriage dowry. Hinde was fortunate to be introduced to a man attractive to her, and by all accounts they were a striking couple. As their grandson recalls in his memoirs: "Dov Sadan [the Yiddish literary scholar] told me my grand-

For a discussion of how women write about their struggle against early marriage, see Paula Hyman, "East European Jewish Women in an Age of Transition, 1880–1930," *Jewish Women in Historical Perspective*, ed. Judith Baskin (Detroit: Wayne State University Press, 1998), 277–278.

11. See ChaeRan Freeze's *Jewish Marriage and Divorce in Imperial Russia* (Waltham: Brandeis University Press, 2002), 11–20. As Freeze shows, Hinde was far from alone among Eastern European Jewish youth in learning suddenly that she risked being engaged. In Moyshe Leyb Lilienblum's memoirs, he recounts how he woke up one morning when he was only fourteen to discover that he was engaged. Similarly, Puah Rakowski only learns that she is a promised woman when she is told that her groom's grandmother is coming to inspect her later that day. As Rakowski lamented (14), "A girl did not even have the audacity to oppose the match that her father had made for her."

12. By contrast, two of her sisters married at the age of fourteen. As Melekh Ravitsh writes of his mother's relatively late marriage: "In those times [to marry at twenty] was to be considered an old maid. But she was not an old maid because she was beautiful and well educated. She was an *iberklayberin*, one who is selective in her choices." Melekh Ravitsh, *Dos mayse-bukh fun mayn lebn*, v. 1 (Buenos Aires: Tsentral-farband fun poylishe yidn in argentine, 1962), 19.

father was of Sephardic origin, one of those Jews who came to the east through Turkey ... He did in fact look very oriental. He was dark-skinned, with dark eyes, and as a young man he had black curly hair... As for my grandmother Hinde Rosenblatt, who was tall and beautiful and had almond eyes, Sadan thought she was a *shiksa* [a Gentile]."[13]

The text underscores that Hinde's marriage to someone attractive to her and who shared her modern sensibilities was lucky when compared to the commodification of young Jewish women that dominated her world. Descriptions of her being physically examined for false teeth by a potential mother-in-law, tested for proper temperament by being asked to quickly disentangle a spool of thread, or warned to stay out of the sun so as not to develop freckles that might damage her marriage prospects show the degree to which the destinies of Jewish teenagers were determined by their parents and the dominant values of the traditional community. When Hinde first overhears that she might become a bride at the age of eleven, it is not surprising that her fantasy of marriage is terrifying: a vision of her husband with a dark beard and sidecurls and herself with a shaved head and the traditional wig. Early marriage, in her mind, signified not only the end of childhood, but a threat to her education and enlightenment.

At times Hinde's world seems so thoroughly Jewish that readers might forget that it was the Jews who were on the political margins of society, not the Gentiles. Even within Jewish society, however, the myth of national unity had unraveled by the late nineteenth century, as economic and social stratification took their toll on Jewish harmony. This is most acute in an episode describing how one of Redim's wealthy Jews colludes with the non-Jewish authorities to humiliate her grandfather. The period this memoir covers, then, was one of cultural, economic, and political transition and challenge.

By the time the memoir breaks off in its descriptions of local Jewish life around 1900, the economic situation of Galician Jewry was in decline. Concerted efforts on the part of Poles and Ukrainians resulted in frequent boycotts against Jewish merchants, including the establishment of agriculture cooperatives meant to get around having to trade with Jews and the cancellation of alcohol licenses for Jewish merchants. When the estate her father leased was no longer economically

13. Yosl Bergner, *What I Meant to Say: Stories and Travels as Told to Ruth Bondy* (Tel Aviv: Hed Arzi, 1997), 14–15.

viable, he was forced to find other business opportunities. World War I led to tremendous dislocation and suffering. Galicia was occupied by Russian forces, and remained on the front line in the Polish-Ukrainian war. The disintegration of the Hapsburg monarchy in 1918 led to further turmoil, as both the Poles and the Ukrainians accused the Jews of collaboration with their opponent. Poles celebrated their victory over the Ukrainians and the incorporation of Lemberg (renamed Lwow) in the reconstituted Polish republic with a pogrom that killed seventy-two Jews in November 1918.

Hinde and her husband Efrayim remained in Redim, now Radymno, through the interwar period. The economic security Hinde knew as a child grew increasingly precarious as the local economy shrank due to industrialization and business shifted to larger manufacturing, business, and cultural centers. Efrayim experienced the collapse of several businesses, and he was constantly forced to seek out new opportunities to support himself and Hinde. In the larger Galician centers Polish anti-Semitism led to restrictions on Jewish admission to universities. Efrayim suffered a stroke and paralysis at the end of his life, dying in the summer of 1939 just prior to the Nazi invasion of Polish Galicia later that fall. When Nazi forces occupied Radymno, they gave its Jewish residents two hours to leave their homes on the eve of Yom Kippur, 22 September 1939. Hinde—then sixty-nine years old—fled across the border to the Soviet Union, where she relied on the support of local family, Jewish writers who respected the creative accomplishments of her sons, and whatever assistance her children could send from abroad. When Germany attacked the Soviet Union in 1941, Hinde's fate grew desperate. In her last plea to her sons for help, delivered through the Red Cross, she wrote: "I am very weak … It will soon be too late." Hinde Bergner disappeared in 1942. She is believed to have died together with her brother Mordkhe at the Nazi extermination camp of Belzec. She would have been seventy-two. The text's abrupt end in mid-sentence symbolizes the many millions of Jewish lives robbed of their creative potential. There is evidence that Hinde had been growing increasingly confident as a writer. For instance, as we near the very end of the memoir, we discover that she sent different versions of the same episode to her sons. These textual variations (an example of which is included in this translation) show an author intent on polishing her writing to produce the best possible narrative. Had she had more time, Hinde might have left us more pages about Galician Jewry as it entered the twentieth century, with valuable information about how the age of nationalism and ideology played out in small Polish towns.

Hinde's decision to begin writing her memoirs in 1937 and their posthumous publication in 1946 owe much to the encouragement of her sons, the Yiddish writers Melekh Ravitsh and Herts Bergner. They must have been aware of her loneliness—one of her sons was already dead, the other two had left Redim long before. Perhaps they believed that this endeavor would prove therapeutic to their mother in her old age, and also provide them with a record of the family history. What they could not have imagined, however, is how engaged she became with the project, and how quickly she emerged as a natural storyteller. From 1937 through 1939, Hinde regularly mailed her sons her handwritten memoirs on foolscap paper. In the first paragraph of the memoir, she admits that writing imaginatively allowed her to fill the emptiness left by the absence of her three children. In more than one respect then, Hinde Bergner's efforts are not dissimilar to those of the most famous Yiddish woman memoirist, Glikl of Hameln (1645–1725), whose memoirs were also intended for her children, and were also written over an extended period (1690–1719) at a remove from the events described. Just as Glikl reveals that her project is motivated by a need for comfort "to distract my soul from the burdens laid upon it,"[14] so does Hinde begin her memoir with the admission that "on long winter nights, I often sit alone beside the stove. My thoughts stray far away to my children and grandchildren, who are spread out over this wide world. I long to be close to them, to tell them about the childhood that floats so vividly before my eyes, as if I were once again a young girl." Like Glikl, Hinde saw herself a mother first and a memoirist second. Both offer more a snapshot of community than an intimate self-portrait. Yet, in Glikl's memoirs one still feels the heavy influence of the Hebrew ethical will or *tsavoe*, a traditional literary genre through which parents leave behind moral instruction and wisdom to encourage their children in a life of piety. By contrast, Hinde's

14. *The Memoirs of Glückel of Hameln*, trans. Marvin Lowenthal (New York: Schocken, 1977), 1.

post-traditional perspective has none of Glikl's moral expectations and acerbic self-judgment.

Hinde Bergner's memoirs also position her as the matriarch of one of modern Jewish culture's most creatively accomplished families. She and her husband Efrayim had three sons. The oldest, Moyshe (b. 1892), was a painter in the Land of Israel before his suicide in 1921. Hinde's youngest son, Herts, was born in 1907. He was a Yiddish novelist and short-story writer, who lived in Australia until his death in 1970. Hinde's second son, Zekharie (b. 1893), achieved the greatest fame. He changed his name to Melekh Ravitsh (based on his favorite Yiddish poet Melekh Chmielnitski and Yanko Ravitsh, hero of a story by Yiddish writer Lamed Shapiro) when his first Yiddish work was accepted for publication under that pseudonym. Melekh Ravitsh left Redim as a young man for Vienna, then moved to Warsaw, where he emerged as one of the most significant young Yiddish modernist poets of the interwar period. He helped direct the Yiddish expressionist movement *Khaliastre* (The Gang), co-founded Poland's most important Yiddish literary journal, *Literarishe bleter* (Literary Pages), and served as secretary of the Yiddish Writers' Union in Warsaw, before leaving Poland in the mid–1930s for Australia, and then Montreal, where he died in 1976. Apart from his many volumes of modernist Yiddish poetry, Melekh Ravitsh was an important translator (he translated Kafka into Yiddish) and literary critic. A strict vegetarian and Spinozist early in his career, he brought a cosmopolitan panache to the world of Yiddish, and later his home in Montreal emerged as the cultural address for Yiddish in Canada. *Mayn leksikon*, his idiosyncratic, multivolume lexicon of Yiddish writers based on his personal encounters and impressions, and his extensive memoirs round out one of the most significant careers in Yiddish letters. Melekh Ravitsh's daughter, Ruth Bergner, is a talented and well-known dancer in Melbourne. Ravitsh's son Yosl Bergner is one of the most acclaimed modernist artists of the State of Israel, whose life's work was celebrated in 2000 with a retrospective exhibition at the Tel Aviv Museum of Art. Ruth and Yosl spent extended periods during childhood with their grandparents in Radymno while their father worked in Vienna and Warsaw.

Hinde Bergner's memoirs establish her as a creative force in her own right. Yiddish readers have long been aware of a number of talented artistic families—such as the brothers Zalmen and Avrom Reyzin, the siblings Israel Joshua Singer, Isaac Bashevis Singer, and Esther Kreitman, the father-son teams of Hillel, Arn, and Elkhonen Tsaytlin, and the scholars Max and Uriel Weinreich. All the same, I am aware of no other Yiddish-speaking family that has left us published memoirs from three successive generations. Hinde Bergner's memoirs were followed by Melekh Ravitsh's *Dos mayse-bukh fun mayn lebn* (The Story Book of My Life, 1962–1975) and Yosl Bergner's *What I Meant to Say*. In these volumes by Hinde's son and grandson, the influence of her writing is evident. Both constructed their memoirs in a style approximating hers—a series of very short episodes, each of which contains the description of a specific event, person, or scene. Although Melekh Ravitsh, in his original foreword to this book, apologized for the fact that his mother was "hopeless" in terms of style, owing to the fact that she was not familiar with the genre of the memoir, in reality his own memoir owed much to her simple, episodic technique.

As early as 1914, at the very beginning of his poetic career, Ravitsh dedicated the first of several poems to his mother and childhood in Redim, testifying to their significance in his artistic development:

> *In zilbern vayse, shtralndike kindhayts-teg,*
> *Flegstu—o, tsarte froy—oft oyftsuraysn*
> *Di tir fun kinder-shtub, un in dayn yung gemit undz vayzn*
> *A zilber-velt; un flegst undz, kinder, nemen oyf a vaytn veg,*
> *Un shpiln zikh mit unz un lakhn vi a zilber-glekl–*
> *Yunge muter–*
>
> *Shoyn lang oys kind, mayn yugnt lesht shoyn oykh, mit libe raykh*
> *Un veytog. Di shotns tsien zikh shoyn lenger oys un zinken;*
> *Di ershte, zilber-fedim in di shlayfn dayne—muter—vinken.*
> *Shoyn zingt ver a farnakhtlid, farbenkt un fun yener zayt taykh–*
> *Zorgnfule muter–*
>
> *Ful mit mider benkshaft vartstu oyf mayn yunger menlekhkeyt,*
> *Mayne orems zoln shtarkn zikh un zoln zikh tsu di baderftike*
>   *shtrekn.*
> *Vi bay likht-bentshn vestu di mide oygn mit di hent fardekn,*
> *Un langzam, zikher geyn—shtolts fun zin, fun dray bagleyt–*
> *Alte muter–*[15]

---

15. Melekh Ravitsh, "Muter" (Mother), *Di lider fun mayne lider* (Montreal: Yidisher folks bibliotek in Montreal, 1954), 28. For other poems of a sim-

(In silver-white, radiating days of childhood
You—delicate woman—often tore open
The door of the children's room, and reflected
A silvery world in your countenance; you would take us,
    your children, on a distant path,
And play with us and laugh like a silver bell–
Young mother–

Childhood is long gone, youth is already extinguished,
    with rich love and sorrow,
The shadows extend longer and sink;
The first, silver-filaments in your brow—mother—wink.
Now an evening song resounds, nostalgic, and from the other
    side of the river–
Mother full of worries–

Filled with tired longing you wait for me to reach young
    manhood,
For my arms to grow strong and extend to the needy.
You will cover your tired eyes as when blessing the candles,
And slowly, confidently depart—proud of your sons,
    accompanied by the three of us–
Old mother–)

The poem's image of Mother as source of all beauty comes up against the speaker's guilt at having abandoned her to pursue a career as writer in the distant city. The poem suggests that her earthy goodness and dignity provide an ethical model that serves as a link between Mother's world of the *shtetl* and the more cosmopolitan, secular varieties of Yiddish creativity embraced by her son. Decades later, Ravitsh's memoirs offer intimate portraits of his mother that seem to pick up chronologically where her memoir leaves off. Ravitsh's recollections credit Hinde with awakening his artistic soul and providing him with a rich cultural legacy critical for his emergence as a writer.

> Neither my father nor my mother had good voices, but they loved to sing...Whenever they were in high spirits they would recall a melody and sing it together. My father's voice was warm, beautiful, and melodious, though a bit raspy because of his smoking ... He was also

ilar sort, see "*Di mishpokhe Ravitsh*" (The Ravitsh Family), "*Redim, mayn shtetele*" (Redim, My Hometown), and "*A man fertsik yor hoybt on a briv tsu zayn mamen*" (A Forty-Year-Old Man Begins a Letter to His Mother).

a wonderful whistler, but he was ashamed to whistle in public because it was not appropriate behavior in respectable Jewish circles …

Apart from the melodies and songs that my parents both shared each also had a private theme song to symbolize life.

My mother's life-song was based on a Polish tune about a bee that falls in a stream. It begins to drown and calls out for help. The bee cries out until her help-buzzes and frantic wing-flappings are overheard by a dove. The dove rescues the bee on its white wings. Immediately thereafter the bee stings the white dove. The dove falls into the water and the bee peacefully flies off on her heavenly ways … What kind of song was it?—a folksong, an art-song, perhaps a cabaret or operatic ballad from the nineteenth century as was the custom—I don't know. I still remember a portion of the Polish lyrics … I remember the melody clearly. It sings inside me always, and it sings out from me in moments of despair when I am nostalgic, longing for all that's distant, and when tears start to fall without any reason, and perhaps because of many reasons all at once …

Mother had the habit of sitting for hours, retreating inside herself in silence. At the end of these silences she would suddenly burst out in song, singing her melody. It gave her the courage to stand up and do what she had to do …

When mother sang her tune for the last time she was all alone. She wrote to me about it in 1942—when she was already in the Nazi-occupied sphere, when her hand was already shaking and her only way out was a quick and easy death. How death came and when, I do not know the precise truth. But I am certain that her ash is mixed with the earth of Belzec and her soul has risen … on the wings of her melody … into the heavens above Belzec.

In one of her last letters, she writes: I composed a melody all on my own and sing it when I am sad and alone. I sing it to you, my sons, and I imagine that you can hear your solitary mother. It is possible that she provided her melody with extra notes in her last months, weeks, days, minutes. The melody is certainly based on her life-song. And if she was still alive when she was locked into the gas chamber, her melody was with her there, and expired together with her last breath of gas.

Such is the story of my parents' life-songs that I inherited from them—and that I have already given to my daughter and son as an inheritance.

Only people die, not melodies. They are stronger than time, stronger than the walls of gas ovens.[16]

16. Ravitsh, *Dos mayse bukh fun mayn lebn*, 325–330.

Hinde's influence was just as palpable in her grandson Yosl's creative development. Years later, when he was starting out as an artist in Australia, Yosl did a series of paintings of Radymno based on his childhood recollections, which included images of his grandmother and her hometown. In his memoir he reveals that when he first came to Warsaw to rejoin his father, he pined for the simple familiarities of Radymno and his grandmother's tenderness. An artistic career spanning more than sixty years remained punctuated by surrealistic images of family and household objects once found in Hinde's home. The empty picture frames, expressionless faces, and ritual spice boxes in the form of churchtowers are but some of the repeated motifs in his work that tell a story of personal loss and historic rupture caused by murder and the destruction of a childhood sanctuary. Yosl insists that his childhood memories of Radymno are an essential inspiration to his creative work: "Once, Audrey and I took an Israeli boat from Canada to Israel and I sat on the sunny deck and drew Radymno all covered in snow, and at the window, a little boy. Some sailors came by, saw what I was sketching and couldn't understand: What was this? They looked at the endless sea surrounding us: Where was the snow this man was painting?"[17] He goes so far as to credit his grandmother with introducing him to drawing: "She would draw me Pegasus, a winged horse, and that too can be found in my paintings."[18] Yosl's fondness for his grandmother was so strong that he named his daughter Hinda in her memory.

When Hinde Bergner did not emerge from the ashes of World War II, her sons decided to publish her memoirs in book form as a memorial to their mother. In his role as editor, Melekh Ravitsh gathered the manuscript together (portions of it were scattered in Canada and Australia) and made three textual changes. First, since Hinde never imagined that her memoir would be published, it was Ravitsh who chose the opening line of the memoir for its title. Second, Ravitsh himself divided and provided headings for the little narrative episodes in the manuscript. Last, and most significant, Ravitsh excised material from

17. Bergner, *What I Meant to Say*, 32.
18. Bergner, 24.

two episodes of the manuscript, a total of nine paragraphs. These excised sections concern rather sensational details about her brother's marriage and her niece's children. In light of the catastrophic loss suffered by Eastern European Jewry in the Holocaust and owing to the fact that some of the characters mentioned in these episodes had survived the war, Ravitsh must have felt that these paragraphs unnecessarily revealed family intrigues. Unfortunately, the paragraphs he chose to excise reveal Hinde Bergner as a sharp critic of character, and a juicy chronicler of family mischief. These excised pages are here restored to the memoir. Neither was included in the original Yiddish edition nor in the Hebrew and German translations.

Though Hinde's sons write in their foreword that the memoir has "no social or scientific value," it is my hope that they will be proven wrong. As Melekh Ravitsh writes in the introduction to the second volume of his own memoirs: *"Zikhroynes zaynen eyn shlisl tsu a neshome, ober eyn neshome iz a shlisl tsu a sakh neshomes"*[19] (Memoirs are one key to a soul, but one soul is a key to many souls). I hope that this translation of Hinde Bergner's memoir may prove one such glimpse into the soul of Galician Jewry.

19. Ravitsh, *Dos mayse-bukh fun mayn lebn*, v. 2 (Buenos Aires: Tsentral-farband fun poylishe yidn in argentine, 1964), 10.

Dedication
by Isaac Bashevis Singer*

This is not really a preface but a love letter to the writer Hinde Bergner, murdered by the Nazi villains in 1942 or 1943. When I first read *On Long Winter Nights* more than thirty years ago, I was smitten with a peculiar love for Hinde Bergner, for her wonderful style, for the richness of her Yiddish, and for her deeply human, womanly, and Jewish perspective on people, the world, and God. Generations of Jewish women are given a voice in this book, some chapters of which the writer barely completed. I am filled with regret that she did not manage to finish her memoirs. But that which she has left behind bears witness to the fact that this woman possessed a serious literary talent, a talent and a sweetness that she passed on to her gifted sons and to her blessed grandson Yosl, the highly acclaimed painter.

Art does not emanate solely from the individual. It comes from an inheritance. It is refined over generations. It seems comical that all the defects that Melekh Ravitsh points out in the introduction to this, his mother's book—those for which he begs forgiveness from readers and critics—are actually its highest qualities.

This is an intimate work without any literary pretensions written by a mother to her sons and grandchildren. And perhaps that is why everything in it seems so alive. Its language pulsates from her pen. Like all true art, this book is rich in information, full of details about the Jewish *shtetl* in eastern Galicia, Jewish livelihoods and Jewish clothing. Everything is poured into the mix: piety and enlightenment, wealth and poverty, rootedness and exile, deep sadness and joy in life.

The illustrations in the book provide the work with special charm. I frequently mention Hinde Bergner in my articles about Yiddish literature. She easily could have been the Glikl of Hameln of our era had she had the time to complete her memoirs. But she has left behind a

---

* Isaac Bashevis Singer handwrote this dedication in 1981 for the Hebrew translation of Hinde Bergner's memoir. Yosl Bergner provided me with a copy to translate for the present edition.

treasure nevertheless. I am very thankful to my dear friend Yosl Bergner for these pages of Jewish history—the history of a family of spiritual
aristocracy, of a multi-talented mother and grandmother, of a murdered daughter of Israel, of a physical and spiritual beauty.

On Long Winter Nights, a little book that contains a great deal, is
a literary gem and ought to be translated into all languages.

Isaac Bashevis Singer
6 January, 1981
Miami Beach, Florida

A Word from the Brothers Who Are Publishing Their Mother's Family Memoirs

This collection of family memoirs by our beloved mother Hindzie Bergner—daughter of Blime and Yoysef Rosenblatt—which we are publishing in a limited edition of several hundred copies has no pretensions of being a literary work. Nor does it presume to have social or scholarly significance. When our dear mother was recording her memoirs exactly as they appear in this book, she could count on one hand an audience comprised entirely of her closest family.

Mother was born on 10 October 1870 in the *shtetl* of Redim (in Polish, Radymno), a town on the shores of the river Rada, which flows into the Soen (San), located between the two larger cities of Yerslev (Jaroslaw) and Pshemish or Premisle (Przemysl), which both also lie along its banks. Of the 4,000 people in our town, half were Jews. Sandwiched between two larger cities, our town was always trying to emancipate itself from moldy, old-fashioned ways of life. At least once a week half of Redim would find itself either in Yerslev or in Pshemish—respectively a quarter hour and half hour away by train. Except for a three-and-a-half-year interruption during World War I when our family belonged to the category of "refugees" and lived in Vienna, mother lived all her life in her native town. Her furthest travels were to Warsaw, Vienna, Lemberg, Cracow, and Stanislav. On 23 July 1939, the seventh day of the month of Av, our father Efrayim (born 1866), son of Zelig Bergner, departed this world. He died exhausted after an industrious life of a thousand private little ventures, none of which had ever made him rich, and a thousand and one communal responsibilities that had earned him the love of local Jews, especially the poor and downtrodden.

According to a bulletin from the Red Cross, our mother was still alive in 1942 in Pshemishlani (Przemyslany) near Lemberg. That is all that we know. When our town was occupied by the Nazis in 1939, she crossed over to the Soviet side, where she lived in Rava-Ruska (Rova-Russkaya), then in Pshemishl, and lastly in Pshemishlani. She turned to the Yiddish writers in Lemberg for help and they assisted her from their own scant resources. For this we express our thanks. As far as we know, the writers included the martyrs Alter Katsizne, Yehoshua Perle, and Avrom Zaynfeld (an activist at the YIVO Institute), and the survivors Rokhl Korn and Israel Ashendorf. In Pshemishl, she lived with the Gutt and the Lev families, who are mentioned in these pages. In Pshemishlani, she lived with the Laks family along with her youngest brother Mordkhe, who is also mentioned in the memoirs. She probably lived by selling off those remnants of her jewelry and silverware that she still had with her from happier times, those that had not yet been sold or pawned in darker hours. The real wealth in our family once belonged to our grandfather, Yoysef Rosenblatt. Until the tragic day of 22 July 1941, her sons sent help whenever and wherever possible.

After August, 1942, every trace of our mother disappeared in the sea of pain, blood, and death that flooded Europe from one end to the other. Her last words, communicated through relatives in Switzerland, were: "Send help quickly. I am very weak. It will soon be too late."

The idea that Mother write her memoirs came from her sons. They recognized from the style and writing of her letters that she had literary talent, and they knew that she harbored literary ambitions. She would read for days on end in three languages: Yiddish, Polish, and German. When her sons suggested—and already fairly late, in 1937—that she ought to put her memoirs to paper, she applied herself to the project with gusto. In the end, she realized her dream. She wrote without shame. Before, whenever her sons discovered her notes or even her free-verse poems hidden in some book, she blushed like a child who had perpetrated God-knows-what sin. After she began writing her memoir, she joyfully wrote to her sons about how Father had cut long pieces of paper for her "exactly like those used for real manuscripts," how he purchased fresh ink and pens for her, and how he used to tell her with loving mockery: "So, Hindzie, it's destined that our entire family should consist of writers. In the end, I too will become a writer. In the meantime, show them what you can do."

She wrote the memoirs over a one-and-a-half-year period with significant interruptions. She would send on every few pages to her sons. When they wrote back telling her to continue because the work was good, she was in Seventh Heaven.

But she was helpless in terms of her form. She had no model for this type of memoir, and she did not know what to eliminate or what to emphasize. Since she was writing the memoir for her sons, she did not see the need to describe the people we already knew. When her natural literary and descriptive talents diverted her from the simple, episodic narrative she thought that memoirs ought to comprise, she apologized. She took to stylizing her writing by reworking it; a couple of those multiple pages describing the same episodes accidentally fell into the hands of her sons. They will be included in both versions.

Once, in 1938, our mother became fed up with the entire project. She felt somewhat foolish: "There sits an old lady who writes and writes." Despite this, in 1941, just before Hitler's invasion, and in her seventy-first year, she wrote to one of her sons from Pshemishlani: "I feel that I will be able to write much more because it is only now that I have come to understand humanity. Still, I am greatly disturbed. I do not even have a corner for myself. It is spring already but we are still in a deep winter and I am blue from the cold." There could be no more talk of writing.

In an earlier letter, she had written: "I composed a tune for myself. I sing it whenever I am deeply sad and lonely for you, my sons. I imagine that you hear your solitary mother." At that moment, one son was 4,000 miles away, another 12,000.

In flight, she took along the books her sons had written: "Your poems, your stories give me strength to live and to hope that we will see one another again."

Why are we publishing these memoirs just as they are? Respect for our mother demands it—that, and a mystical feeling. Just as she felt that we could hear her melody from thousands of miles away—we want to imagine that she can see our achievements from the eternity in which she now rests together with six million of our sisters and brothers who perished along with her in the sea of Jewish tragedy.

And there is another reason. An entire world, a Jewish world lies in ruins, destroyed, and even the ruins are being dissipated by the human desire to forget the past. So we are rescuing a fragment of beauty from the ruins, polishing it, and giving it a modest corner in the palace of our glorious Yiddish literature, the eternal living museum of Jewish life over the last centuries.

We call special attention to two figures who are mentioned in the memoirs, the figures of our two great-grandfathers, born at the end of eighteenth century: Moyshe, mother's grandfather, and Yitskhok, father's
grandfather. The former was a simple man. Mother, in her refinement,
refrained from mentioning that his nickname was Moyshe Murze
(Moses the Slob). She only hinted at the romantic escapades of this
glorious rascal. Let us complete the picture. Our step-great-grand-
mother Malkele had a previous husband with whom she had lived in
a "*szlaban*," a toll-house. Our great-grandfather, who was secretly in
love with Malkele, gave the young couple some advice on how to make
a little extra money. Maintaining two separate toll-houses would allow
them to double their income. When our first great-grandmother died,
our great-grandfather came to an understanding with Malkele's husband, who was something of a simpleton. So Malkele became both a
rich woman *and* our step great-grandmother, the wife of a husband
almost a half century her senior. They had character, those Jews of
bygone days. The rest of the story is very lovingly described by our
mother, who, for reasons of good taste, transformed the divorcee into
a widow ... so that this beautiful, courageous, romantic episode should
never be forgotten by our family. There was nothing in our great-
grandfather's behavior toward his second batch of children, younger
than the first by forty to fifty years, to put his good name or even his
surname to shame.

Our great-grandfather Yitskhok was a completely different kind of
Jew, as was our father's entire enlightened family. During tense marital
moments, our father—a man of passionate temperament and passionate goodness—would remind mother: "Don't forget whence you
came, don't forget your grand-father's name."

If we have inherited a dash of artistic talent, it certainly comes from
our mother. Her beautiful, almond-shaped eyes observed the world
and saw everything. She would often have to excuse herself in the middle of talking business or during a family get-together so that she could
vent her laughter in another room. This would always enrage our
father, who was ever tactful and well-mannered. But mother could not
restrain herself because she had noticed something comical in one of
the merchants or relatives or friends. She also had artistic talent. When
we were children, she would cheer us out of our most heartfelt weeping

with horses that she evoked with two or three quick strokes of the pen. Those horses—and also winged horses, Pegasuses—are still before our eyes, as in childhood days.

In her youth, in keeping with the spirit of the times, Mother put on a little snobbish affectation. She used to call herself "Henrietta" and not Hindzie, her Yiddish name. But when her sons became passionate Yiddish nationalists—in opposition to the extended family, whose younger generation had almost entirely assimilated into Polish or German culture, and boasted more than one instance of apostasy—she immediately dedicated herself to the ideas of her sons. She quickly came to understand that the Yiddish language meant Yiddish and not "daytshmerish"—Germanized Yiddish. She began to correspond with her sons in pure Yiddish, and not in German or in Polish as she had done until then. But father remained a *maskil* until the end. Using the Yiddish alphabet, he would write such things as: "*Mein lieber Sohn, hiermit theile ich Dir mit, dass ich mit grossem Vergnugen Dein liebes Schreiben empfangen habe,* etc."

We are publishing these memoirs in the name of all three of our mother's sons. We include our oldest brother who, on 26 March 1921, willingly took leave of this world. He was born on 12 October 1892. He ran away to the Land of Israel in 1910, where he was a pioneer for ten years, among the first. He served in the Jewish Legion under the British Mandate and was awarded medals of distinction. In 1920, he came for a temporary visit to Vienna to round out his education, and after discovering a talent for painting, he lost his will to live. Our mother never ceased to adore him and never erased him from among the living. That is why we are including him.

For months before his suicide, he painted a different self-portrait every day—painted and tore it to pieces. Only a few of them survived. The final one was the most frightening. It was painted a day before his death. Our brother was known in Palestine as Moshe Harari (earlier, Haroni). It was under this name that he served in the army and signed his paintings. He published a little under this name in Hebrew, and before that, in Polish, mainly artistic, impressionistic writings about the life of the pioneers in the Land of Israel prior to the First World War.

We are also publishing several reproductions of paintings by Yosl Bergner, one of our mother's two grandsons, for whom these memoirs were also intended. Blime Ruth, who will be mentioned together with him, is Yosl's older sister—she is a dancer. She inherited her musical talent from her mother, a singer—Fanye Bergner-Ravitsh. Several pictures of our *shtetl*, family pictures and a facsimile of her handwriting also appear in this volume.

Dearest Mother! Many of your dreams will remain forever dreams, but your dream to write has been realized ... Now you are also an author like your sons. We envy your restraint, your ability to portray a person in two or three strokes, especially since we require word after word to express ourselves. Perhaps this lengthy introduction is evidence of this.

Melekh Ravitsh—Herts Bergner
Montreal, Canada—Melbourne, Australia

November 1945

P.S.: Half of the manuscript was in Australia, the other half in Canada. We recopied the memoirs before publication. The spelling of the original already approximated the modern orthography of the YIVO Institute for Jewish Research. We were forced to divide several of the longer sentences into shorter ones. Like most people from Galicia, our mother tended to long sentences. But the Yiddish language cannot bear this. The style is our mother's. The changes are minimal. But we did not find it necessary to retain Mother's orthography because the memoirs have no scientific value from a linguistic standpoint. A facsimile of part of the manuscript is included. Not wanting to overly distort the manuscript, we retained Mother's chronological chaos, but offered section headings for the sake of readability, thereby automatically instituting some order. We eliminated three or four pages of the text because they contained overly personal stories about members of our family.

M.R. – H.B.

On Long Winter Nights …

On long winter nights, I often sit alone beside the stove. My thoughts stray far away to my children and grandchildren, who are spread out over this wide world. I long to be close to them, to tell them about the childhood that floats so vividly before my eyes, as if I were once again a young girl.

I run to school …

I still feel the chill of winter mornings when I wrapped myself in a big, checkered shawl with long fringes and stole out of the house to school. I hear Father's angry voice from once upon a time when he used to scold me: "A big girl ought to have business on her mind rather than confusing herself with such foolishness." He had no use for a child philosopher. It was dark outside. I slinked out quickly so that no one at home would notice me and stop me from leaving.

The school was locked. I would either wait or ask the caretaker if she would open it for me. I was very industrious. I believed then that I could become something extraordinary. It was dark in the schoolhouse, so I lit a candle that I secretly brought with me from home. While I waited, I embroidered a big goat-hair shawl. I had to be careful doing such "practical" work, because nothing would have saved me if Father had caught me doing such a thing, not even if I had quickly managed to throw the shawl under the table. Father always said: "A seamstress—I can have for a pittance. You should be watching over the storehouse and making sure people are not stealing from me." Despite this admonition, I did what I wanted. I both studied and watched over the storehouse, and I was awarded prizes in school.

My father loves me but he does not allow me to study …

When I finished primary school in Redim, my father decided that I had enough formal education. Now I could do his accounting. He loved me dearly, because only six of his fourteen children had survived. I was the youngest of his three remaining daughters. My two older sisters were already married. Whenever father needed to travel somewhere, he left all his money behind with me. And it was no small amount— around ten thousand Rheinische, or Gulden.

I begged my parents to allow me to go to Yerslev during vacation to stay with an aunt (one of my mother's sisters) because I had a cousin my age there. They refused. I was very angry, and I ran away to my sister Mirl because I felt comfortable with her. She had many children. The entire incident saddened my father, and he tried everything to get me to forgive him. Father and I journeyed together to Yerslev, where we met with the Rebbe Bunem-Mendl. He wanted the *rebbe* to bless me so that I would no longer be angry with him. When the *rebbe* asked me why I did not want to make up with my father, I answered: "My father beats me."

Marketplace in Redim
(the long structure is the old town hall, built in 1800, the building with the tower is the new town hall, built in 1896)

Naftoltshe

After that incident, I was never angry again. Father loved to retell the story. He rejoiced in my "becoming good." I was rewarded for this. Father enrolled me in the *kheyder* that one of my cousins attended. I really liked the boy. He wore a blue suit with gold buttons. I gave him four Kreuzer as a gift. I still remember that my uncle said to my father: "Make a match in childhood and look for a big dowry later ..."

The boy's name was Naftoltshe. He once accompanied me from *kheyder* to help me choose a new hat. It was a white, plate-style hat with blue ribbons and a zig-zag pattern. Doctor Reys's daughter had hats just like it. Years later, whenever one of my brothers fought with me, he used to tease me by mentioning my fondness for Naftoltshe.

My grandmother Etl, my mother's mother

My maternal grandmother was Etl Frayfeld. When my grandfather, Mordkhe Frayfeld, was still alive, the couple lived in Shtshitne (Szczitno) and owned an inn. Whenever my father wanted to tease my mother, he would remind her that she was from some backwater village. I remember my grandmother Etl very well, even though I was only six or seven when she died. She died at her youngest daughter's home in Pavloshov. Grandmother Etl was thin, of average height, and she had a pretty face. Her eyes were already pinkish due to her age. She resembled my mother. I never knew my grandfather Mordkhe. He died very young, and my grandmother Etl was left without financial support. She had no sons, and of her four daughters my mother was the richest. Therefore, she lived with us most of the time. I still remember one of her dresses that she left hanging in the attic when she traveled to see her youngest daughter in Pavloshov, where she suddenly died. The dress remained there in her memory. Whenever I went up to the attic with the washerwoman, I stopped to gaze at the dress with admiration. It was made of black silk and had big, blue glistening leaves. It was a dress fit for a princess, with an internal corset made of fishbone that laced up around her figure. Over her bosom she wore a neck-kerchief made of canary-yellow muslin, onto which were embroidered bluish-black velvet ribbons. Underneath the skirt she wore a small crinoline.

My grandmother Etl looked majestic on *Shabes*, the Jewish Sabbath—the only time she wore the dress along with a small cap instead of her weekday wig and a hat. The cap was made of a shiny silken brocade. On her brow lay a golden velvet bow with lace, and a flounce of pleated violet lace dropped down just below her ears. The cap resembled the type of hat that the wives of rabbis still wear today. Long diamond earrings set in silver hung from both sides of the cap, and she wore a headband strung across her forehead like a crown. The headband was adorned with checkered pearls and diamonds.

A tragedy about a hen and her chicks

When my grandmother was dressed in her Sabbath-best, I forgot entirely about the pain she caused me in the incident of the hen and its little chicks.

We were a country household. Though we lived near the city, we had our own fields. We cared for several cows, and from time to time a calf was born and we would raise it too. I loved the farm, and often I used to go with our Gentile servant Ruszka to fetch hay from the barn for the cows. This did not please my father and he used to send me off to the granary to supervise the unloading of the grain.

Once, when I was standing in the granary next to the stable, I had a thought. I asked our old Ruszka, who was busy milking the cows: "Listen Ruszka … Maybe we should sit the big, speckled hen on the thirty eggs we found in the attic of the barn." She answered: "Yes … Yes! …"

We sat the speckled hen on the eggs in secret, so that nobody would know. It cackled without pause because it wanted to hatch them. I was overjoyed when chicks began to scratch their way out of their shells, and out came twenty-two chicks. I fed them cheese, and I bought wheat for them with my pocket money. I arranged a bed for them in a big sieve in the kitchen. My grandmother slept in an alcove near the kitchen. She was not pleased that the chicks were spending the night next to her in the kitchen. One evening when the hen and her twenty-two chicks were already sleeping in their sieve underneath the bed, and when I was fast asleep, my grandmother ordered our Jewish maid Soshe to take the hen and the chicks out to the woodshed that was next to the barn in the yard.

In the morning, as I always did before I got dressed, I ran into the kitchen to see my little chicks and to give them something to eat. I looked for the sieve. Unable to find it, I woke up our maid and screamed: "Soshe, where are the chicks?" Half asleep, she answered:

"In the yard, in the woodshed." She told me that Grandmother ordered her to remove them. Breathless, I sped off toward the shed. I was stunned. There, sticking out through a crack in the door, I saw the wing of the mother-hen. I tore open the door of the shed and froze in my tracks at the sight of the disaster. A headless hen, only its wings remaining, and not a trace of the chicks. Not even a feather. I asked Ruszka, who had helped me set the hen on the eggs in the first place, what had happened? Only she could understand my heartache. I told her what I witnessed in the shed. She said to me: "Oh, my little princess, I noticed it before you. The polecat strangled all the chicks and your grandmother is responsible!"

I forgave my grandmother for this incident long ago.

My grandfather Mordkhe, my mother's father

As I told you I never knew my paternal grandfather Mordkhe from Shtshitne. He died young. He ran a tavern in Shtshitne, and later in Povloshov. He left behind no sons, only daughters. My mother, the eldest of his daughters, observed the anniversary of his death every year. On the anniversary of Grandfather's death, his *yortsayt*, she distributed money to the poor. She hand-made the memorial candles that she divided up among the houses of prayer.

My mother's goodness and strictness

People still talk about how kind my mother was to the needy when she was a young woman. They also talk about how she used to go on foot every Friday from Shtshitne to Yerslev to bring the *rebbe*, Reb Shimon, a twenty and a flask of whisky for *Shabes*. He was very poor. Reb Shimon was the father of Bunem-Mendl, the *rebbe*. Once, on a cold and snowy Friday, she was barely alive when she arrived at the *rebbe*'s with her charity. She managed to hand him the flask with her frozen hands before almost fainting. Reb Shimon was deeply touched by her kindness. With tears in his eyes he said to her: "Young lady, you will not be in need of anything for the remainder of your days. You will know no hardship. I give you my blessing that you will be a very rich woman."

My mother had deep concern for the poor. Everyone was the same to her, Jew or Gentile. She gave food to all who were hungry: for Leyb the tailor, a freshly baked loaf; for old Sore, a bowl of soup; for Abale the tailor, a stick of butter with some cheese; for our rabbi, Reb Mendele, she had me bring a little sour-cream or buttermilk with big chunks of butter mixed in—nourishment for his weak heart. But she did not spoil her own children. For example, if I dared come home tired from reciting *slikhes,* the penitential prayers, and wanted to sit down to rest, my mother would address me by my Sabbath name: "Hindele, you're tired already?" Laughing out loud was expressly forbidden. She referred to the reading of Polish or German books as busying oneself with *treyf-poslen,* heretical garbage, and she would order me to read the *Tsena-urene* in their place.

I flee to Yerslev—to study ...

When I finished school, Mother wanted to tie me down to housework immediately, while Father wanted me to become involved in his business. But I had a powerful young will to learn. I fought with my parents until I was allowed to realize my dreams.

My father loved me very much, but he did not want to hear any more about my going to Yerslev to study. I pleaded with him, I embraced him, I kissed him, but it was useless. My mother might have been persuaded, but she was something of a religious zealot, and she feared that if I experienced life in a modern city I would not grow up to be a pious woman. But I remained focused on a single thought—how to devise a plan to steal off to Yerslev.

While I was lying awake one winter dawn, I heard the noise of a carriage approaching Mikhalovke, the name of our estate. It was still very early. In our household, people woke early during the winter, around four or five o'clock in the morning, to study, pray, and eat a breakfast of hot cereal and freshly cooked potatoes by the light of a candle or lantern. Suddenly, while I was lying there thinking and listening to the sound of the carriage driving onto our property, an idea occurred to me. I threw myself out of bed and ran to the coachman. I gave him a bundle of twenty-five "quarters"—that equals one Rheinisch Gulden. I pleaded with him not tell a soul, and to drive me directly to my aunt's house in Yerslev. While my family was busy eating, I ran away.

Father brings me back to Redim

I stole away from home with the intention of realizing my dream to learn, to become educated, and to take piano lessons. This was my lofty ideal. And even though I was very young at the time, I remember

promising myself that I would never impede the desire of my own children to learn!

Upon hearing of my escape to one of my mother's sisters, my Aunt Shtern in Yerslev, Father quickly figured out that I was planning to enroll in school there. He immediately came after me and pleaded with me, both gently and angrily. He argued: "Yerslev, Shmerslev ... What's the point? You have the potential to be a very good accountant. You can be my right hand in business and at the same time you can study with the school director Shtshenkevitsh. As a gift, I'll give you the grand piano the magistrate Kraft left behind, the one in the barn garret. As for money ... I'll give you as much as you want so that you can buy a real piano just like your friend Yultshe, Doctor Reys's daughter. Hindele, your mother says that I'm responsible for all this because I spoiled you. I'm begging you, come back, let's go home. And if you want to, we shall pay a visit to the *rebbe*, Bunem-Mendl, so that he can recite a blessing over you to obey your parents ..."

I did not agree with Father's plan to go to Bunem-Mendl's, and I also did not want to go home with him. We argued for a long time until I noticed that Father's voice was cracking. And when I turned to look at him I saw tears falling from his eyes. His face was contorted and ashen. Moved by his tears, I began to cry too. As I kissed his work-worn hands, I promised to come home with him. Father had toiled hard in

Row of houses in the residential quarter of Redim

his youth. He used to measure all the different types of grains for peasants into "quarters"—twenty-five-kilogram wooden casks that resembled small barrels. Iron bars in the form of a cross lay across the open tops of the casks. Standing in the dust, he was able measure out more than a hundred quarters of grain a day.

I begin private lessons

I abandoned my Yerslev plan, but I was no longer prevented from taking private lessons. I began to learn French with a respected teacher, Glik was his name. I bought myself a book, and I managed to learn just enough to read and write a little French. By the time I was able to combine a few words and ask my mother in French to buy me a new hat, the teacher moved away from Redim and the book was abandoned in the attic.

I become my father's "right hand"

I became my father's assistant. I oversaw the mixing of grains to prevent them from spoiling. I would go to the barn to check on the handlers who were supposed to bring the threshed grain home from the fields. I used to count the *kortses,* the 100-kilogram bags of grain, as they were loaded onto the wagons that took them to the train. Summer and winter, I spent my days in the granary. On one occasion I remember how ashamed I was standing in the granary with a shawl over my head, all dusty, my lips and nostrils black as soot. Just then, the son of a merchant from Yerslev arrived with the rye cart to receive his delivery. He was well-dressed, very handsome, and seemed to be an intelligent young man, perhaps even with formal academic training. Lowering my eyes to the ground, I thought to myself how different I—the daughter of the wealthy Yoysef Rosenblatt, proprietor of the Mikhalovke estate—would have appeared had I been allowed to remain in Yerslev … Another incident occurred while I was on my way to supervise the distribution of grain in the warehouse. I was bringing Makhle—the Jewish woman who oversaw the early morning threshing of the wheat—a warm jug of coffee with two rolls for lunch. Suddenly, the civil engineer who lived across from us approached me and introduced himself. "I know that you are the daughter of the estate owner Rosenblatt." He regularly greeted me after that encounter. Once he dropped in after returning with his horse and wagon from Mikhalovke. It was ten o'clock in the morning and we were all sitting around the table eating a warm meal, soup with crushed groats. I still remember how surprised the engineer was, and how he asked me: "Lunch already? … So early? …" I was very embarrassed. The engineer certainly noticed this and after that, whenever he ran into me, he would ask: "Is lunch ready?"

Makhle

Makhle was a prime example of a Jewish women who aged before her time. Her face was all "plowed up," full of wrinkles. Two long black ribbons hung from her glasses. She always tucked a copy of the *Korbn-minkhe* under her arm, and draped a big shawl over her peasant coat that she fastened with a straw belt. She looked like an old peasant woman. She stood in the barn all winter, supervising the counting of sacks of grain for threshing, and praying without pause, almost by heart.

Makhle and her husband Efrayim, who was also prematurely old, had their own little house with a straw roof and a large garden not far from our barn. Everything was white as chalk in their home. Makhle scoured everything with bundles of straw and sand. Her garden was filled with all kinds of wondrous plants. On Sundays, all Redim would buy vegetables from her. If someone dared to tear out even one blade of grass or to tread on a bed of vegetables, she became enraged. We got along well. Whenever I came over to buy something, I didn't follow her into the garden to watch over her. As a result, she always chose the nicest corn for me. Her garden was superbly manicured. It had not one superfluous blade of grass, and the footpaths were clean and shiny. Flowers grew even along the borders of the paths. She had worked on all of this with her aging hands.

Makhle proposes a match for me …

"You know," she once said to me, "you are already a beautiful young woman. You are very attractive. You have even caught the eye of the property supervisor. Your father ought to have proposed a *shidekh* for you already …"

Upon hearing such words from Makhle's mouth, I lowered my eyes and did not want to look in her direction any more. All of a sudden the black knotted shoelaces tied to the wire arms of her glasses, her wide, flat nose, and the black mole on her lower lip made her seem like a witch to me.

Matchmaking, Matchmaking

I do not know whether Makhle was responsible for this or not, but from the moment she uttered those few words, *shidukhim* did not cease coming my way day or night. Matches were proposed for me only, even though one of my brothers was two years older. Once, returning home from the granary, I managed to overhear my father say: "Yes, I can immediately offer a dowry and even arrange a wedding within two weeks …" When I learned of Father's decision to finalize an engagement for me so soon, I did not enter the room but went to the children's bedroom instead. Unable to hold back the tears that were choking me, I burst out crying. I was maybe eleven years old then, and I was still used to stealing away to my schoolmates' homes to play. Even though my father kept me busy working for him throughout my childhood I nevertheless managed to borrow German and Polish books, in secret so that my mother wouldn't find out. I read them at night in bed by the light of a wax candle. And all of a sudden, here came this scarecrow of marriage raising its terrifying head. Inconceivable—I imagined my husband's beard and long *peyes*, his side-locks, while I pictured myself wearing a *shaytl* instead of my beautiful long, blond braids. Wringing my hands, I mourned my lost dreams and my ambition to acquire a higher education so that I would surpass all my girlfriends.

Itsik Pipek, the shadkhn from Pshemish

Every *shadkhn*, the traditional Jewish matchmaker, was my enemy. I did my best to evade them. I couldn't even look at them. One matchmaker, Itsik the Bellybutton or Itsik Pipek from Pshemish, always brought a pocketful of prospective grooms with him. Mother received him nicely with strong whisky and a snack, and inquired about possible matches. It was lucky that Father was always away on business and never had any time. Had he not been so preoccupied, I most certainly would have been a bride by twelve years old, because Mother left no stone unturned. When prospective bridegrooms and their families came to visit, she would ask me to dress nicely, enter the room, and allow them to examine my ability to write Yiddish, Polish, and German. Itsik Pipek the matchmaker was a red-head with a white, moonish face, and light-blue eyes that were always smiling because he was so pleased with himself. This broad-shouldered little Jew with a long body and short legs looked like a potato. I assure you that he did not bother me. He was lazy and never pressured me. I was able to trick him easily into leaving our house by persuading him that he should go over to my friend Sheyndl's, where he would get a nice welcome and payment for his expenses. He immediately obeyed me, and put on his black caftan, the one with the long curved side pockets. A tobacco-stained handkerchief dangled from one pocket, and the green tassel of a long pipe hung from the other. And off he went, to discuss matches with other families. But other matchmakers caused me great heartache. One of them, desiring to ingratiate himself with my father, tattled on me by telling him that I spent time outside in the sun, and that I would get freckles on my face that would cost him dearly ...

The matchmaker from Nemirov, Fishl Koyletsh

Fishl Koyletsh, a nickname meaning braided eggbread, was a local man who married a woman from Nemirov. Though not a matchmaker by profession, he used to come to Redim to buy flax. He proposed a match for me with the son of a wealthy estate owner from Nemirov. Time and again, he tried to convince my father: "I don't understand ... a rich Jew and a good family ... what's the delay?"

My parents began to inquire into the match. The father of the groom was Eliezer Shtorkh. His family was known to be stingy, but that did not seem to matter much. But when my father heard that the boy's name was Yosl, the same name as his, he didn't want to hear another word about the match. Father put a dark end to the whole affair, asking the matchmaker how he, a Jew from Redim, could propose such a match. Of course, I wasn't sorry at all even though I had never set eyes on the bridegroom.

"Bokser"—a third matchmaker

And before we had a chance to catch our breath, a third matchmaker came along. He was a tall, near-sighted Jew. Whenever he wanted to look at me, he would wipe his glasses and turn his long body so quickly and wildly that I couldn't contain my laughter. Sometimes, when he ran into the living room, he would hit his head on the chandelier because he was so tall. He was known as "Bokser," carob-head, because of this. Oh, how this matchmaker is engraved in my memory! He worked mightily, traveling, running, writing, telegraphing—all without our knowledge. He enticed us to come to Pshemish. First, only

Father went, and then he forged my father's name on a telegram invit-
ing the rest of us to come too. Well, don't ask how much heartache I
caused my mother, the poor thing, when she told me where we were
going. She begged me sweetly and angrily, she kissed me, and she
cried: "Why won't you even consider it? These people have come from
as far away as Gorlits. Should we put them to shame? I am begging you,
don't be so stubborn. You are a grown girl already." Tears flowed from
her eyes. The tears helped, and I went with her. When Mother and I
arrived at the station and met some acquaintances, it occurred to me
that they all knew why I had traveled there and my face reddened with
embarrassment.

We arranged in advance to meet at the residence of the Gutt family
in Pshemish. But when I arrived, the family from Gorlits was not there.
Great confusion ensued. All our trouble had been for nothing. I was
pleased with the matchmaker's misfortune. Father was very angry at
him for making us all travel there just to "dance on ice." He told him
that he had lost faith in him. If you think that the wild matchmaker just
forgot about the match, think again. He started from scratch until he
managed to bring the entire group—the father, mother, grandfather,
grandmother, and son—to our home. And he carried out the "inspection" with all the fury of his zeal.

The first inspection

If I recall correctly, the whole thing occurred on a beautiful warm summer day in June at eight o'clock in the evening … It is still light. I am
standing by the open window with a jasmine branch in my hand,
observing the countryside. I breathe in the fragrance of the jasmine.
The variety of spring aromas that filter through the window are intox-
icating. Suddenly, I see the "Bokser" driving the whole world toward
our home. I quickly close the window and run into the children's room
from which I can observe the entire affair. The big lamp and the lights
in the chandelier are illuminated. The green, cashmere Sabbath cover
with its glistening gold embroidered flowers and gold tassels is
unfurled. The tablecloth, which is made from the same fabric as the
cover, is also laid out over the wide drop-leaf table. The guests are
received and I am called in. At first, I shoot a glance toward the window
to see whether my friends are peeping through the open blinds, and I
bashfully look at the boy who is standing and talking to my brother.
I see a pale, sickly face with a black curly beard that is quite bushy

already. The boy looks like an established householder. I don't look at him any more. I attempt to overhear the nature of the language in which he is conversing with my brother. The boy's mother is speaking to me. She looks into my mouth to see whether I have any false teeth, she inspects me to see whether my coloring is off or whether I have an artificial eye. She asks me to disentangle a spool of silken thread. Apparently, she wants to test me, to see whether I am quick-tempered.

And the years flew by

I thanked God when they left without coming to any type of arrangement. I heard my father say that he was suspicious of the boy's sickly looks. He was already at work on a new match. In the meantime, the years flew by with matches that never quite materialized. My mother, poor thing, was greatly troubled by this. She wanted to lower the wedding veil over me. She was such a good, observant, pious woman.

Daring to go to the theater in Yerslev

The following happened once on a beautiful frosty night: the snow squeaked underneath our feet. The entire town—the houses, the roofs, the trees—were all bedecked in white. Icicles, brittle from the afternoon sun, hung from the roofs. The sky glimmered in magnificent splendor with its sparkling stars. All of nature seemed to be preparing for a festive ball. Even I was happy and warm. Still not a bride! Freedom! One of my girlfriends came over and proposed that we go to the theater in Yerslev. A nice play was being performed there. The Jewish farm manager from the village of Ostrov offered to take us there in his handsome sleigh with its splendid, beautiful horses. I did not want to make my friend beg for long. I slunk over to the closet quietly, not wanting anyone to see, and I took out my winter coat. As if to spite myself, I accidentally overturned a bottle of Jamaican rum. Ignoring what had happened, I snuck over to my friend's house anyhow. A number of girls my age were already gathered next to her house. The farm manager was preparing his sleigh. He said that he would wait for us in Yerslev until the play was over, and in the meantime he would go with his sleigh and horses to an inn. Suddenly, when we were just about to set out, my mother appeared like a bolt of lightning. She grabbed my sleeve with both her hands and dragged me home. She screamed at me so loudly that everyone could hear. "This little missy is so impudent that she thinks she can ride away without her parents' permis-

sion!" The entire way home, she beleaguered me: "You greedy glut-
ton! You wanton girl! When everyone goes to sleep you dare to go on
a little trip!" And what would have happened had she also known that
I was on my way to the theater? With my eyes lowered in regret, I went
home with Mother, thinking to myself that I had committed God-
only-knows what type of sin in my desire to travel.

For a long time, I refused to forget the degree to which Mother
had shamed me. I could not look my friends in the eye for quite some
time unless one of them approached me first. Could Mother have been
right? Today, I too would do anything to protect my granddaughter.
One of my friends even said to me then: "Your father should divorce
your mother for the shame she caused you in front of so many people!"
But my mother told nobody at home about what had happened, and
I certainly did not dare open my mouth. Later, I was convinced that
Mother had been correct. When an amateur theater company staged
a show in Redim, Father bought a ticket specially for me. He waited
up for me until I returned home to ask me whether I had enjoyed it.

My grandfather Moyshe, my father's father

My dear children, I would now like to tell you something about my
grandfather Moyshe, your great-grandfather, my father's father. I
never knew my grandmother Sime, grandfather's first wife. She had
heart trouble and died young, leaving behind only four children: three
daughters and one son, Yosl, my father. I say "only four" children
because my mother gave birth to fourteen children and one of my
father's sisters, Khaye-Sore, had eighteen children, including two sets
of twins. My grandfather Moyshe Rosenblatt was the complete opposite of my father. Father was considered sensitive and he had a weak
heart. In his youth, he had to go to special centers for treatment. He
never failed to tell us how hard he worked when he was a young man,
standing for entire days in the dust until he became sick. He used to
drink weak tea, which he called "tea-water." Next to his bed he had
several pairs of boots, old and new, and two or three pairs of felt shoes,
as tall as leather boots. When he put them on, he would walk back and
forth to make sure that they weren't pinching his feet. When he was
aggravated, he always loved to say: "I swallow my pride and make
nothing of it." But Grandfather Moyshe was quite a character. He was
always in a good mood, and he loved to enjoy himself with a friend by
treating him to wine or beer. He could drink several glasses of wine,

and then beer as well. In contrast to him, I laugh when I am reminded of how my father, after a meal or on a hot day, would send for just an eighth of a liter of beer. He would drink it one sip at a time, with breaks in between. Grandfather Moyshe was a show-off and a very healthy one at that. He had wide shoulders, big conspicuous hands, and a festive face. He was always upbeat and ready to do anyone a favor. He had a habit of agreeing in almost every sentence by adding: "Indeed, indeed." His clothes were not much different from those of Jews like him today. He always tucked in his clothes with the help of a wide belt. His gait was wide and confident. He held a nice tobacco pouch in his hand and he always was prepared to treat someone to a pinch of snuff.

My grandfather takes me to an exhibition in Pshemish

My grandfather was curious about everything. When I was still a little girl, he took me to the great exhibition in Pshemish, which Father, a much younger man, had no interest in attending. When we arrived in Pshemish at eight in the morning, we went to a tavern and he ordered two big portions of hot fish, one for me and one for him. I could not eat so early in the morning; my stomach was upset the more I ate. But Grandfather urged me: "Eat, eat, you will be hungry running around the entire day at the exhibition." After the fish, Grandfather drank a shot of liquor and, after that, half a glass of beer. He took his big bag in his hand and said to me: "Let's go, it's getting late!"

We had taken along one of my classmates from Redim, Dintshe Mol. She was already waiting for me by the entrance to the exhibition. We held each other's hands and marched in together with Grandfather, gawking at many remarkable things, like the recently invented machines. We were especially interested in the sock machine. The young woman sitting at the sock machine knit like a demon. All she had to do was to touch the machine with her hand and socks poured out in leaps and bounds. We thought that the young woman was a magician.

Grandfather soon appeared. He had run into an acquaintance and spent his time examining more important-looking things than we did. I still remember how much we enjoyed buying soda water all on our own until Grandfather interrupted by calling after us: "We'll be late for the train. Let's go. That's enough already."

Grandfather gave me his tall leather bag to carry. It must have weighed fifty kilograms, and was bigger than I was. I was dressed in a pale-blue, silk embroidered dress. I wore a straw hat that had long violet velvet ribbons hanging down from it, and pretty gloves made of fine cloth. I was a little embarrassed to walk next to Grandfather. I strode alongside my classmate, who was also nicely dressed. Dragging that bulky piece of luggage almost drained away all my pleasure. It was still light outside, a beautiful hot July evening, and many people were rushing home, while I was tossing up dust everywhere, dragging my grandfather's bag. Some lost their temper, others laughed. I must have appeared quite ridiculous.

My grandfather is punished with a thrashing

My grandfather had once been punished with a thrashing. My father used to repeat this story passionately because he had a grudge against one of our town notables who was responsible. I also knew the man. He still has a grandchild living in Redim. This Jew, M.B., was supposedly one of the great intellects of the town in his time. He was one of the most feared householders in Redim because of his arrogance. He did not care to converse with many of the other townsfolk, and whenever someone entered his house, Jew or Gentile, on business or on pleasure, the visitor would have to hold his hat in his hands. He was not nearly as rich as he was arrogant. His family fraternized mainly with the Jewish intelligentsia, or as much of one as there was at that time. Wherever he went, he had priority, both in business matters and honorifics. He was also a member of the city council. Outwardly, he was a very handsome Jew with dark-blue eyes—almost black really—a nice black beard, and an authentic Semitic nose. But from beneath his long whiskers, a cocky smile spread over his handsome face with such arrogance that whenever you stood in his presence you would recoil and not know how to behave—perhaps bow down before the lord and king? Jews tried to avoid him. But my grandfather was known as a stubborn man. And so one day he haggled with him over the rent from several taverns. This honorable man, this refined Jew, thought that he would teach my grandfather a lesson so that the next time Grandfather would remember whom he had chosen to challenge. He wanted to show Grandfather just what he was capable of and how much power he had. Without any warning or explanation, he summoned Grandfather before the town magistrate. My grandfather was escorted through the entire market by two policemen and he was chained next to the magistrate's door. In the presence of everyone, they draped my proud grandfather across a bench and placed dirty, damp rags on his naked body. When this honorable man, this refined, noble Jew, uttered the command, the policeman whipped my grandfather exactly twenty-four times. My father was not a vengeful person. But he could not forgive this arrogant, haughty Jew for the disgrace.

My grandfather remarries in his old age

Grandfather was not affected by this disgrace. He did not lose his spirit or strong will, and the townsfolk had no less faith in him than before. He did not differentiate between common workers and the wealthy. He ate and drank, bought and sold, with everyone without differentiating between them. When his first wife, my grandmother Sime, died, he soon remarried a woman he had known from the time before Grandmother's death. She was his employee at a tavern on the road not far from Dobromil, and Grandfather used to visit that tavern more than any other. I knew Grandfather's second wife, my step-grandmother, quite well. She died while fleeing the Great War. I never knew my grandmother Sime because I was born after her death. I want to tell you that my grandfather was a real "connoisseur"; he paid no attention to matters of family descent. His second wife was a tailor's daughter and her mother was a poor widow. He even took in her mother to live with them. If I recall correctly, I think that my step-grandmother was also a widow. But she was beautiful, and strong as a brick wall. She had a medium build with wide hips and a large bosom. She had an alabaster-white face, a nicely carved nose with black, almond-shaped, laughing eyes, and a mouth full of healthy white teeth. Grandfather began a new, youthful life with this wife. She bore him four daughters and a son. He provided for his wife and these children very well, leaving them several houses with gardens and a number of fields. He left nothing to his children from his first marriage. He claimed that his first priority was providing for his younger children. "This is what I am doing because this is the way it has to be."

My grandfather's inn with the three facades

Grandfather's inn, the one with three facades, was a source of great heartache. It was a corner house that stretched right across the road. In the central square there was a bar, a restaurant, several stores, and Grandfather's inn. Anyone driving into the square could drive through the inn straight out onto the road that led to the train station.

There was a kind of passage directly through the building. Whenever I passed through, there was always the smell of garbage and horses. Nevertheless, the inn was a good money-maker. In one of the rooms attached to the inn lived a man called Shimele Nusbaum. He had a wide, well-groomed, red-silvery beard with a long, pointed, hooked nose, a big belly, and strong, fleshy red hands. This man sued my grandfather. He argued that the house belonged to him, so he did not have to pay rent. The legal process extended over a long period of time. I was only a little child but I still remember the fear and terror that he caused, this Shimele "Processnik," a derisive term used to indicate his litigious nature. He paid some *shkotsim*, local thugs, to attack my grandfather at night. He also paid off fake witnesses from Sokolov, who falsely testified that the house belonged to him. For this reason, to this day residents of Sokolov bear the pejorative nickname "Sokolov witnesses." Grandfather left the building to his younger children. These children, now grown up, sold it to Lazer Bliher.

The blaze at the inn and revenge

The inn was very run-down. One winter, in full daylight, it burnt to the ground. Today, many tall, multi-storied houses stand in its place. The fire consumed half of the town's homes, leaving many poor people without a roof over their heads. The daughter of the proprietor of the house where the fire first broke out was so frightened that she fell ill. She was already a married woman and she had been visiting her parents. Her terror resulted in a depression that persisted several years until she died, leaving behind two young boys. In the same fire, another tavern went up in flames—the place belonging to the aforementioned arrogant Jew. But he was already dead by that time, that smug Jew who caused my grandfather to endure a public whipping.

The noble widow

The "honorable" Jew's wife, also very attractive, was a dominating woman with pretensions to noble ancestry. She was alive at the time of the fire, and the poor thing was forced to shuffle between rented apartments. As if that was not enough, she was also paralyzed. Her grandson's wife refused to take her into her home, even for payment, despite the fact that her grandson virtually grew up in her home. The grandson's wife was afraid of her reputed strictness. People used to talk about the way she behaved and how she rebuked her maids. If a servant-girl was boiling noodles and one fell onto the floor, she would say to her: "Tell me, is this noodle too ill to behave like all the other noodles?" The grandson's wife was too frightened to allow this woman into her home. But her grandson admired and respected her, and he remained proud of his family lineage. Had it been up to him, he would have taken in his grandmother.

I remember that when she was a widow, one of her married sons lived with her. She still had a noble appearance and people respected her. She was of average size and plump enough, with a pale face, black, energetic eyes, and a beautiful proud Jewish nose. When she could no longer put on her *shaytl* on her own, she wrapped a shawl around her head to show off her nicely shaped ears and her long silver earrings inlaid with diamonds. The majestic power of her former beauty was not lost. Your father and I used to visit her often. She could never understand her son's pregnant wife, who used to wear baggy dresses and wide blouses. With arrogant self-confidence, she would complain: "I never changed my wardrobe. I wore the same clothes and corset, and even though I was pregnant, I never loosened the corsets or the laces. I gave birth to fourteen beautiful children, all without a blemish." Since her son's wife feared taking her in to live with them, she had to live with strangers. Your father and I would visit her often because she was one of his aunts.

I give birth to my first son—Moyshe

I recall the birth of my first son, Moyshe. It all started Saturday night after the Sabbath ended. The pains were not that great so I did not pay too much attention to them at first. All women have children, I told myself, and so will I ... I wanted to go through this alone, without the help of a doctor. Unfortunately, the birth pangs continued through Wednesday evening and by then, because of the pain, I was getting out of bed all the time and running around like a madwoman with my long, blond hair flying all over the place. This was going on at my parents' home, and the old midwife, Sheyndl, decided on her own to send for Doctor Reys. By that time, I was hoarse from all my screaming. If that was not enough, it was a hot September day and all my strength was sapped. I screamed at the doctor, bargaining with him that if he put an end to all of this, I would reward him with anything as thanks. But he was relaxed and patient. So as to leave no stone unturned, Mother ran to all the synagogues. Aunt Sime Berglos, as your father called her, stood next to the bed praying. Her eyes were damp and both her arms were extended toward the heavens, pleading with God and crying. She looked like a holy woman to me. Even though it was the forceps that did the trick in the end, Aunt Berglos was a great support. Whenever people in town needed advice or wanted a piece of jewelry appraised, they knew to go to Sime Berglos.

The early childhood of my second son, Zekharie

When you, Zekharie, my second son—whom I suckled myself and weaned at the tender age of seven months—fell sick with an intestinal illness, both town doctors were away at a physicians' conference in

Hinde Bergner's sons Moyshe (right) and
Zekharie (Melekh Ravitsh), 1900

Lemberg. We went to the military doctor. He was a very lucky find and prescribed good medicine—a glass of boiled water with a beaten egg-white and a teaspoon of cognac. He told us to mix everything and give the child a spoonful every hour. The second remedy was to return to breast-feeding the child because everything else would harm him. Aunt Sime Berglos did not at all agree that we should resume breast-feeding again because she believed that this would result in your having a poor memory down the road. But we paid no attention to her and I ran around searching for a wet-nurse because six weeks after weaning all my milk had dried up. This happened smack in the middle of harvest time. I asked the wet-nurse who had worked for my sister Laytshe (and who was already suckling a much bigger child) to help me. We lowered the blinds so that nobody would see. Zekharie, you returned to breast-feeding. But I had to work at it diligently until you were so starved that you caught on. From then on, I nurtured you with the water medicine. Later, I finally succeeded in finding a wet-nurse with a child. I employed this wet-nurse with her child until you were healthy again. A few years later, I teased Aunt Berglos because you had an excellent memory. When you were two years old, you could recite several poems by heart, and even when you were only eight months old, you could call the wet-nurse by her name—Hanke.

My children, later I will try to tell you about my school years. But first, I want to tell you what my parents told me about their lives, their youth, and how they lived until the time they managed to buy a house by using a fake, non-Jewish name. I will try to describe that house.

A little about my parents' first apartment, around the year 1850

My father always repeated how he came to Mother with a dowry of only 150 Rheinisch Gulden, and lived in a tiny room in the home of a non-Jewish butcher. His table was made out of a barrel with a noodle-board on top. His chairs were two buckets. If that wasn't enough, Mother used to tell us about how they were ordered to take in a soldier for a few days from time to time. Without asking her, a soldier once took a plate and put pork on it. Mother, who so strictly observed the Jewish dietary laws, had to remain silent.

Hinde Bergner (right) and Zekharie (Melekh Ravitsh)

My parents' own home

A few years after his marriage, Father was the only one in town to receive a draft notice because, even back then, Grandfather was considered to be quite rich. For the price of five hundred Rheinisch, Grandfather bribed an official and the draft notice was forgotten. When Father began to involve himself in commerce, he was very fortunate and did quite well. He very much wanted to buy his own house. This was very difficult in those days because a Jew did not have the right to buy a house of his own. He purchased one under a Gentile name he assumed. In 1914, during the Great War, the house burnt down. I will never forget it. I regularly dream about it and the barn full of animals. In particular, I think about Gniadule the cow that used to turn her head whenever I entered the barn. And Tsharnule, the black cow that had only one horn. Ruszka, our Gentile maid, used to sing a song about orphans while she was milking the cows and I used to climb up to the garret to gather the eggs from the chickens.

Chickens and pigeons

Whenever I was angry, I used to hide in the attic of the barn so that nobody could find me. A big hut stood in the middle of our yard. I used to play there with my girlfriends. Whenever I fed the chickens, pigeons flew over from the neighboring school. I used to sneak grain (so that Father wouldn't see) from the granary to feed the pigeons. From his window, the school teacher noticed what was going on in our courtyard. He saw how devoted I was to the pigeons, and so he brought me several nice storybooks to read.

A description of our house

In earlier days our home had been a courthouse with several prison cells. The iron bars remained. The house was very big. Two barred windows faced out onto the courtyard and two more faced the street. It had a little vestibule with a balcony, and a door facing the street. That part of the house was used for business. As a schoolgirl, I used to stand there on market days and ask those who passed by: "*Macie zboze do sprzedania?*" (Do you have any grain for sale?)

Further on, there were two rooms in which my parents lived. There was an alcove with a window that also faced the street. And I still remember that next to the window, where once there must have been a shutter, there hung a rope with a little stick to open and shut it. Father used to stack two chairs on top of each other by the window at night so that if a burglar tried to enter, the chairs would fall over and wake everyone up.

An old story about thieves

While I am on the subject of thieves, I remember a story that my father told on many occasions. In the middle of the night, Father heard a sound coming from outside the window. It seemed to him as though it was coming from the back door that opened onto the neighbor's courtyard. He woke my mother and said: "Blime, listen! Robbers are trying to break in. Go and see!" He was too scared to go himself. As a result of their arguing for so long about who should go first, all the window panes opening onto the courtyard were broken. My parents ran into the courtyard screaming to frighten off the burglars. The next day, one robber, poor thing, complained to another: "You see, Dovid, even the rich can't sleep."

The living room and the chandelier

Beyond the alcove there was a large room that we, the children, referred to as the furniture room. The alcove opened up onto a beautiful, whitewashed living room. It had a spotless floor, which Ruszka scrubbed with straw and sand. It was a shame to step on it. Above the door, there were two large brass pipes, about forty centimeters each. Two brass birds were screwed onto them. Every Friday, before she lit the Sabbath candles, Mother would stand on a little stool and insert the big paraffin candles that she had already lit into the pipes. From up there, the birds seemed as though they were creatures from the Garden of Eden.

A big brass chandelier hung from a beam in the middle of the living room. Several pipes holding the candles rose up from it, and between each pipe there was a brass bird. The room was quite large, and boasted three windows. One faced the little lane and the two others opened out front. The ceiling was low, and seemed even more so because of the beams. When Mother used to recite the blessing over the candles Friday evening and light paraffin candles in the chandelier's pipes, it seemed as though the divine presence itself was there.

Father used to sit at a little table next to the window in that room on Sabbath mornings and pore over the weekly Torah portion, humming a very beautiful melody. I remember the tune to this day.

A book case containing several exquisite shawls

In the living room with the beautiful old chandelier, there were also two book cabinets. The older one, which was yellowing and very solid, had four little glass panes. It contained an assortment of books, including a copy of the *Tsena-urene* with Rashi's commentary, which I used to take out and read every Sabbath. It also contained a small book that had a hand painted along the length of the title page. Above the hand was the inscription "*Hakhmas ha-yad*" (Wisdom of the Hand). Several pieces of cloth were laid out on the two shelves that lacked glass panes. They were shawls that Mother had made as a wedding present for Father. We should pause for a moment and describe these exquisite shawls. They were fifteen centimeters wide, made of thick canvas. Each had individual threads of grass-green silk in a garland embroidered along their entire length. The garland, which consisted of violet flowers, buds, and leaves, was so artistic and the colors were so natural, that it appeared as though they had sprouted out of the grass-green embroidery. If not for the war in 1914 the shawls would still exist. I had wanted to keep them as a way to remember Mother. They were so wonderful. You could have put them in a museum exhibition for people to see. To this day, I have yet to see such magnificent handiwork.

The "Serwantke," a glass cabinet for silver

The second book cabinet was a little darker, with a browner varnish. It was more modern, and stood in the corner of the living room. The cabinet had two large glass panes. One of them was round and extended right across the cabinet. An assortment of silver items was displayed at the top. In truth, the cabinet was designed more for silver than for books, and so we referred to it as our "Serwantke." A crown decorated with a wreath of flowers was carved at the top.

The first round, glass-paned shelf of the cabinet was decorated with blue and white flowered wallpaper. In the middle, a colored ribbon had been tacked down with brass nails with spaces between them. Different pieces of silverware were inserted between the spaces. There were several pairs of silver candlesticks, a large tray that was lent out for the *pidyen haben,* the ceremony for the redemption of first-born male children, and a silver bottle engraved with figures in human form left to us by my grandfather Moyshe. Once, when my mother used that bottle to send wine to the rabbi, he ruled that such a bottle was forbidden in a Jewish home. When Father heard about this, he went to the rabbi to ask him his opinion about the bottle. The rabbi ruled that Father should cut the noses off the engraved figurines on the silver bottle.

The silver "tsits-kley-koydesh"

The silver cover for the Torah scroll was kept on the same shelf. Its design consisted of an ark with gilded little doors that opened and closed, and a silver chain that could be hung over the scroll. We called these our "*tsits-kley-koydesh*," our corolla ritual articles.Whenever a boy started to learn Torah and stood up to give a short explication of the weekly reading on the Sabbath, his family would borrow these items, dress the child in them, and add silver and gold-plated watches to his outfit.

There were also two silver boxes in the cabinet. One was a little tobacco box with deep beautiful engraving. The much larger one was used to hold the *esrog*, the fruit used during the festival of *Sukes.*

The blessing over the esrog and an old bookbinder

I still remember the bookbinder, a dark, thin little man, his nose yellowed from tobacco. He was far from a youngster. He wore a wide black caftan that shone like satin because it was so worn out. He used to twist a silk belt around his hips several times, and tie it in front so that its fringes dangled down. Every year, he borrowed our big *esrog* holder so that he could recite the blessing over the citrus fruit. He never allowed me to take down the *esrog* so that I too could bless it, and he used to yell at me in his dull voice: "No, No! Don't touch it with your hands, wash them first and then I'll hand it to you." When we removed the *esrog* from its fine, thin, white flax, his black, goat-like beard would tremble with fear. He would also wipe his hands in the lap of his caftan before touching it. And while I recited the blessing over it, he would stare at my hands to make sure I was not squeezing it or, God forbid, about to drop it.

The second compartment of the Serwantke, the one with straight glass panes, contained a beautifully bound Talmud. It was purchased for my brother Natan-Neta because Mother had hoped that he would become a rabbi.

Our porch

From the living room, two windows opened onto a long, brick-laid porch. It stretched the entire length of the front of the house, extending past the corridor door and a room with a little window that still had iron bars over it.

I still remember how much I enjoyed playing "*kamer-kamer-hoyz*" with my three girlfriends on the brick porch. We placed four bricks on each square meter and each of us stood on one brick. We jumped from one brick to the next, holding one another's hands, and whoever's foot missed a brick dropped out of the game.

The balcony was very comfortable for both children and grownups. It was big and wide, and protected us from sun and rain. It had comfortable balustrades that we used to sit on. During military maneuvers, the police chief would sit up there and survey the scene. On Sabbath afternoons, it was a very pleasant place. Since our entire family lived very close to one another, all the children and grandchildren gathered there. My mother gave out Sabbath candy or fruit to everyone. My children, you certainly remember the balcony. Zekharie, you remember for sure, and perhaps you too, Herts.

The treasure of the swallows

I remember that there was a small drawer that could not be opened carved into one of the balcony's posts. My friends and I were convinced that it was an enchanted drawer that contained a treasure. We were afraid to touch it. One of my friends said: "Underneath the roof of the balcony, there are a few swallows' nests, and when the birds fly away for the winter, they take something out of their nests and hide it in the little drawer."

Another story about a robber—and maybe even an evil spirit

The little room with the iron-barred window was the children's room that belonged to me and my cousins. I still tremble when I recall what happened to me one hot summer night. The window was open—it had iron bars—but the door of the room was closed and both corridor doors were also shut. My father checked the locks every night and locked the doors. I was sleeping in one bed along with my sister's daughter Rivtshe, a little four-year-old. My brother Neta was sleeping in the other bed. He slept so soundly that you could chop wood over his head and he wouldn't wake up. On that hot, summer night I woke up and sat on the edge of the bed. I wanted to push away the chair that stood next to the bed, but instead I clearly felt somebody's shoulder. Then I heard a "shhh" passing through the room, like the sound of the wind. As if that weren't enough, I heard the main door slam shut. I was too frightened to scream in the middle of the night and my hair was standing on end. However, because I was so terrified I did begin to shout "Neta, Neta!" A miracle occurred—he heard me and lit a candle. Together, holding each other's hand, we went to look at the door. It was not bolted. We searched the entire house, even looking under beds, but we found no one. But since this all happened at precisely mid-night—during the hour of the ghosts—we concluded that it had been an evil spirit. Mother invited a scribe to check the ritual purity of the *mezuze* affixed to the doorpost of the room.

The little room and my mother's stories

In her final years of increasing frailty, Mother used to spend the sum-mer days in our little room so that nobody would disturb her and so that she wouldn't be in anyone's way. The room was cut off from the rest of the house, and had its own entrance. I used to spend several hours with her there each day. She would tell me stories about the years just after her wedding.

Once upon a time … the first train

Mother told me about the time she was preparing to light the Sabbath candles, and was in the process of putting on her satin headband. At first, this was difficult for her to do because she was only fourteen years old. She had to pin the headband to the brown hairpiece and little net. But first she had to pin the black velvet head cap to her shaven head so that the hair band would be held in place. The round jewelry box with the frieze of green leaves—I can still picture it today—was already open with the jewelry all arranged. The bejeweled headband was taken out of its hiding place in the box. It consisted of three rows of wire with big, smooth pearls strung onto them. In the front it had a big diamond broach in the shape of a crown. Along the entire length of the head-band there were smaller diamond chips inlaid in silver. Suddenly, my father ran in all out of breath with a big piece of news: "Blime, did you

hear the whistle? That is a train. It moves without horses. The entire town was there." We were all amazed at the wonder of human inventiveness. To think that a person could now travel without horses. Today—Mother continued with her story—people drive only on wheels. She particularly hated motorcycles because of their smell and noise. She had encountered them first in Carlsbad. She referred to them with an appropriate nickname…

My father's first bride

Mother also told me that once, after her marriage, she went shopping and ran into Father's first bride. Mother was wearing the sweater that this woman had given to my father as a present. His former bride said to her: "Hey, Hey! The first one builds and the second one settles."

In her old age, my mother also used to make new clothes. She used to say that youth itself made young people shine, whereas older people needed to dress nicely in order to be attractive.

Mother referred to the children's room as her "city of refuge." Each year, she would ask God to allow her to enjoy one more summer in it.

My father's cousin, Borokh Berglos, often visited us on the porch. He brought along his wife and children. His wife referred to their son Yankev (Jacob) by a Polish name—"Kuba." When Mother heard this through the window, she was very angry. She said to me: "Isn't Yankev nicer than Kuba? Kuba is such a non-Jewish name!?"

My mother comes to Herts's bris

When I was pregnant with Herts, Mother was already quite sick. She was very frightened, and knew that the end was quickly approaching, though she never said so out loud. But I understood her thoughts. She assumed that since I already had two sons and had not had a child for thirteen years, precisely now, when she was at her weakest, I would give birth to a daughter and name her Blime in her memory. But when I had a son, she summoned up her remaining energy to come to the circumcision ceremony, the *bris*. She dressed beautifully in her Sabbath finery. She wore all her jewelry, a black silk dress, a strand of pearls, and a plush brown shawl over her head. It all suited her so nicely. Even though she suffered from diabetes, she looked regal. Her face did not contain a single wrinkle and her grey-blue eyes shone like the morning stars.

Mother loved Herts dearly and our wet-nurse, a wild spirit, used to bring him to her in her beloved hiding place in the little children's room and run off to visit her suitors.

Mother spoiled Herts and would play with him on her bed for days on end. When she died Herts was only eight months old.

My mother's last blessing over the Sabbath candles

After a number of bedridden weeks, Mother suddenly got out of bed on her last Sabbath eve. She asked us to bring her water so that she could wash, and to bring the red cloth jacket with the black, velvet embroidered collar. She dressed and put on a snow-white, beautifully embroidered petticoat. And as though nothing was wrong with her, she walked unassisted over to the table in the alcove where the candlesticks were standing. She raised a white, silk kerchief and placed it over her white head. She recited a *tkhine*, a private supplicatory prayer, with great emotion, performed the blessing over the Sabbath candles, and returned to bed on her own.

Hinde Bergner's son Herts, Vienna 1915

Mother's last Sabbath and the days of mourning

Sabbath morning, the doctor prescribed cupping for my mother. The procedure required one to light and extinguish a flame over and over. Mother said to me: "Look Hindzie, how the Sabbath consumes my eyes in fire."

In the afternoon, when she was still sitting on her bed in her Sabbath clothing, she said: "Blime has never been a coward. I am not afraid of death." This meant that she had a pure conscience, that she had made her peace with everyone around her, and that she had infused goodness into everything she did from her childhood through to the end.

I remember how Father used to say to her: "Blime, will you leave some down feathers for me too in the Garden of Eden?"

When people came to console the mourners, everyone spoke of Mother's goodness. Nobody was afraid to speak his mind on account of Father. Everyone was free to tell the truth. Some recounted how she had distributed grain to poor vendors before the harvest, and fed the children of poor widows so that these mothers could try to earn a living in the marketplace without having to be worried about their children. In her youth, when she had been able to, she had even suckled poor infants from her own breast.

My parents in their final years

My mother lived seventy-three years. She was sick for twenty. Father felt cheated because of this. I remember how he often seemed absorbed in thought and downcast, and how he quietly used to sing a wistful tune to himself. He sometimes even liked to get into a discussion with a neighbor and hold her hand. After mother's death, father was seventy-some years old. He had children living at home with him who attended to his needs, and maid-servants as well. Even so, he made an effort to remarry, and to a woman far younger than he. He had the first betrothal meeting set up, but the truth of it is that his children interfered.

I remember how Father used to tease Mother and tell her a story about a husband who wanted to trick his wife. He convinced her that she ought to divorce him just for fun and then he would take her back. His wife went along with it and they got divorced. He immediately summoned the matchmaker so that he could marry someone else. But his children bribed the matchmakers and they set up a match that everyone agreed upon and the deal was closed. Both of them were satisfied: the bride, because the children had provided her with a lot of hush-money, and the groom, who was pleased by the prospect of a more beautiful, younger bride. In no time at all the wedding canopy was raised. After the ceremony—when the groom saw his bride without her veil for the first time and realized that it was actually his original wife—he cried out in bitter humor: "But don't you see, I kept my promise. I told you that I would take you back." Whenever he told the story, Father shook with laughter and Mother used to say to him: "Yosl, you would not have succeeded either."

My mother recited the confessional prayers many years before her death, especially in her beloved "city of refuge"—the little children's room. She did not cry and she confessed before several people, including Father, his sister Aunt Khaye-Sore, Melekh the beadle, and me. We were all very moved—I was moved to tears. But Mother was content. Aunt Khaye-Sore said to me: "Don't cry. Confession is a remedy, and your mother will live longer."

My Aunt Khaye-Sore

Aunt Khaye-Sore was a nice, old-fashioned woman. She was like my grandfather Moyshe: always bright, cheerful, hardworking, intelligent-looking, fearless, strong and broad-shouldered. During the week, she wore a kerchief on her head and a broad apron with two deep pockets over her dress. She used to sink her hands into the pockets as if she were soaking them to get rid of dirt. She would come to Father and say: "Yosl, listen to how my Leybush was dragged off by a demon during the night. You know that my devout husband sits and studies during the winter beginning at four in the morning when the entire town is still pitch black and there isn't a light on anywhere. Suddenly, I hear someone banging at the window and he opens the door, goes out, and doesn't return. This lasts for over an hour and I think to myself that he must surely be in heaven. In fact, it was only some drunken landowner who had jumped into my husband's carriage, demanding that he show him the way to a tavern."

One Friday, when I was still a little girl, I remember how Aunt Khaye-Sore called for me: "Come quickly!" She handed me a cleaver and said: "Chop the fish for me because I have to run to the store. I'll give you a honey-cake." That was some honey-cake! A thick, dark loaf—but very tasty. At home with Mother I never would have had such a honey-cake.

Khaye-Sore bedecked for the Sabbath

On the Sabbath, Aunt Khaye-Sore used to put on a satin hair band that had little peaks like a bonnet, and a large brim. Between the hair band and the brim was her headband with long, flat diamond earrings set in silver attached underneath with a cord so that she wouldn't lose them. Over her hair band, she wore a bonnet, a type of lace hat whose front was adorned with three large, dark-red roses. She loved vibrant colors. And descending from the hat, crossing down over the brim, was a bow of white silk lace, tied in back.

Aunt Khaye-Sore used to come visit me when I was already living in my own home, after I had given birth to Moyshe, whom we named in memory of Grandfather Moyshe, her father. She used to take him in her arms, play with him, and say: "*Ty, stary Moszka, ja cię tak kocham.*" (You, old Moses, I love you so much.) And he would ask her: "*Dlaczego ciocia ma taki brudny fartuszek? Niech ciocia da, to go niania wymyję …*" (Why does auntie have such a dirty apron? Auntie should give it to the nanny to wash.) And my aunt would unbutton her jacket and show him: "*Patrz, stary Moszka, jaka koszula czysta i biala*" (You see, old Moses, how clean and white my shirt is).

When Moyshe left to study at the *gymnasium*, she was furious with me. "Why do you insist on making him into a Gentile? Look, I have many sons. All of them are making a living from trade and are able to study and support a family."

Uncle Leybush

Khaye-Sore's husband, Uncle Leybush, was short and not very handsome. He had a thin black beard, and a large, protruding hooked nose. On top of it all, he stuttered. He wore his shirt open in front. It had a soft, wide collar. His pants came down to his knees, and were tied with white ribbons over his white socks and slippers. He wore a large *tales-kotn* with long fringes over which he sported a brown gaberdine with big violet leaves, which he fastened with a black braided cord with fringes. He was a talmudic scholar, the son of Khayml of Nayshtot. Nevertheless, he went off to trade with the Polish nobleman from Lowiec. In the eyes of this nobleman from Lowiec, Uncle Leybush was a holy man. Day after day, the nobleman would send deals his way, consult him in all matters, and buy and sell through him. Every day, he would bring home a gift from the nobleman. In the nobleman's court, he was known as *"nasz rabin Lejbusz"* (Our Rabbi Leybush). Whenever someone in the family was in labor, they would inform Uncle Leybush and send him a *pidyen*, payment to secure efficacy. And he deluded himself into thinking that he really was a *rebbe*. Whenever she thought it could be of use to her, Aunt Khaye-Sore would say: "You know, your Uncle Leybush supports you all through his holiness." And sometimes she would mock him: "God Almighty! I could travel to Lemberg by the time he manages to spit out a word; and that idiot nobleman believes in him as if he were God. He is so crooked and so successful … and to have had eighteen children with him!"

Hinde Bergner's son Moyshe as a guard in Palestine, 1911

Khaye-Sore's children and grandchildren

Khaye-Sore died before the Great War, before our uncle. She was about seventy-three years old. Before her death, she summoned all her sons from abroad by telegram and they all came. Her oldest son is around ninety years old today. He is still energetic and healthy. After his first wife's death, he managed three more marriages and three divorces. This time he wants to divorce his wife because she does not come when summoned—so he tells the rabbi—he wants to divorce her and marry a virgin. Khaye-Sore's oldest son is Hirsh-Neta. He puts on the face of a pious *khosid*. He wears long socks and a black silk gabardine, and he thinks he is a *khasidic* master. He is learned, that everybody knows, but he is also stingy. He never provided his wives with enough to sustain the household. Yet he can devour on his own the large pot of cold potatoes that he prepares for himself two days in advance, or the stuffed spleen that he keeps for two weeks, even during the heat of summer. It doesn't harm him one bit. He does not even bring home guests for the Sabbath. His children and grandchildren send him money from America or the Land of Israel. He is still in business. He lent a lot of money to the local Gentiles, which, naturally, they will never return to him in his lifetime.

All Aunt Khaye-Sore's children are doing well, the grandchildren and great-grandchildren even better, except for her son Joseph Asher, who is a pauper. Despite the fact that none of them completed formal studies, she used to boast that almost all of them at least knew how to study Torah. She had only two daughters. "What's the use of girls?" she used to say, "that's like throwing money away."

She used to joke and say: "I would prefer to go to *Gehinom* than to the Garden of Eden. Whom would I spend time with in the Garden of Eden? Shriveled good-for-nothings like my husband? At least in hell I could meet well-fed gentlemen in step with modern times and enjoy myself."

My oldest sister Mirl as a bride

My oldest sister Mirl was like Aunt Khaye-Sore. She had about eighteen or twenty children. She was married at thirteen, maybe fourteen. She used to tell how her husband, my brother-in-law, was invited as a bridegroom to spend the festival of *Shvues* with us when he was about twelve years old. He performed tricks and was able to jump between

tables without falling. He had called out to her: "Come on, let's play. I see planks lying in the courtyard. I'll make a seesaw for us to ride on."

When the parents of my brother-in-law Avrom-Hirsh (Mirl's husband) consented to the invitation, my parents sent a teacher to Krosne to fetch him. During the course of his visit with his bride-to-be that lasted through *Shvues*, the teacher examined him in Torah and Father gave him a gold watch as a gift. After the holiday, father shipped him back home with the teacher.

Mirl's oldest son, Khayim

After their marriage, and following a series of business failures, Father sent them to live on his estate in Mikhalovke. Their oldest son Khayim, who was my age, remained in town with Grandfather and Grandmother so that he could go to school. When he was a little older, he used to wake up during the winter by candlelight in order to go to school. Once, when he had already been sleeping since four in the afternoon, he woke up with a start and saw that the lamp was lit. It was really only nine o'clock at night. He quickly got out of bed and began to get dressed. We all recognized his confusion, but we let him get dressed, wash, and say his morning prayers. He certainly didn't want to drink coffee, thinking that he was already late enough. He grabbed the lantern and ran directly to school. We didn't let him run far. We called him back once he was on his way and really teased him. He was angriest with me: "You saw all of this and didn't tell me a thing about it being night. You let me get dressed and go to school so that everyone could mock me. I will never play tic-tac-toe with you again and I am going to go to see my parents in Mikhalovke on a *shlitele* (that's the word we children used for sled) because I still have not seen how they celebrate the Sabbath there. And I am going to tell them that I am angry with you and why."

My sister Mirl used to come to town with the entire family and two maidservants—one Polish and the other Jewish—to visit our parents during the Days of Awe. And I was very happy with the "unripe pears"—that's what we used to call people from the country.

Of Mirl's children, Khayim was the most intelligent and refined. He was one or two years younger than I was. We played together and went to school together until he needed a *gemore* teacher. My brother-in-law, Avrom-Hirsh, brought a *gemore* teacher from his hometown of

Krosne, and put him up in his house in Mikhalovke. After that, my brother Mordkhe studied with him.

The black melamed from Krosne

Considering the times—that is, some fifty years ago—the *melamed* from Krosne was already quite enlightened. He did not lead his students toward religious extremism. What is more, in both winter and summer, he would walk around with his students for hours and lead them in interesting discussions. The teacher was middle-aged, but his black beard was already streaked with silver. All in all, he was quite dark, almost like a Gypsy. He was refined and slender. Both his face and his clothes, from top to bottom, were black. His gabardine, his vest, his trousers, his socks, his belt, his cap—everything was black. His nostrils were stuffed with tobacco. His tobacco box—which he had carved himself—was admired by everyone. Although his "blackness" was repulsive, he nevertheless attracted the children with his words. My brother Mordkhe never left his side. He carved a beautiful money box as a memento for all his students.

My brother Mordkhe's tragedy with a saved treasure

For a whole year my brother Mordkhe saved silver coins (or *shiplekh* as we called them) in a special money box. They were a gift from Father to his youngest son—his *"benzkunim."* My dear children, if only I could convey the disappointment of my eight-year-old little brother, who returned home from Mikhalovke after two terms of study, opened his secret savings box with great pomp before Father and the family, only to discover inside it pieces of tin instead of his silver coins. My brother threw himself on the ground, yelling, crying, and threatening to kill himself. He screamed out hoarsely: "Who was the thief, who?" Nobody could calm him down. Father refilled the box with real money, but Mordkhe threw it out and screamed: "I only want the money I saved on my own!" In truth, the savings box was beautifully crafted and the mystery of how to open it was supposedly known only to its owner ...

"Drezes the melamed"—my first elementary teacher

My first teacher was not the most appealing of men. He was dark and small and had a hump both in front and back. We called him "Drezes the *melamed*." Of course, he had a real name, but nobody knew what it was. Whenever I recall his face, I want to vomit. His hair was wild, his forehead was wrinkled, and his eyebrows were bushy and thick. His beady black eyes seemed to laugh apishly. His sprawling nose started out narrowly enough, close to his forehead, but then flattened out over his entire face. He had sparse, yellow teeth, bluish-black lips, and a pro-truding lower lip. Snuff kept falling from his wide nostrils, which extended down to his lower lip. All this really provoked great disgust. But he had nice, healthy children of his own.

The Drezes melamed's assistant

As luck would have it, he had an assistant teacher, who came to our home to recite the blessings with me. Thanks to our Polish maid-ser-vant, Ruszka, who raised my brother and me and spoke Polish with us, I recall the following: I was a little over two years old. The assistant demanded that I repeat the words "*nekavim, nekavim, khalulim, kha-lulim*" [part of a blessing thanking God for the creation of the human body and proper bodily functions]. However, I responded: "*Żebyś zdechl, to nie powiem dwa razy nekavim, nekavim, khalulim, khalulim*" (Even if you were to drop dead, I wouldn't repeat "openings, open-ings, cavities, cavities").

"Moyshe Keke," my second teacher

My second teacher was known as "Moyshe Keke." He also employed an assistant. Moyshe Keke was a big-boned, stout man. His shoulders were bent from always having to stoop with his pointer over prayer books while teaching the children. His face was red, his beard yellow. He did not expend a lot of effort. The most important thing to him was to increase his enrolments. Since he was never angry with anyone, many girls and boys were eager to learn from him. The room where we studied in his home was small and low, without a real floor. His wife had a pit next to the kitchen so that when she cooked potatoes she wouldn't have to go outside to strain them. That one room where doz-ens of children studied was also the kitchen and the bedroom. It was fortunate that they didn't have any children of their own. Near the win-dow that faced a closed alley was a large table where students studied. During the summer, children who had already finished their lessons would walk around in the closed alley, which measured just two square meters. The teacher taught at one end of the table while his assistant taught at the other. Every child studied twice a day. In the evening

before going home, the assistant and all the children would gather in the middle of the room. He would herd us together like sheep to recite the *boyre nefashes*, an abbreviated form of grace after meals. It was also the assistant's job to take us to every woman who had given birth to a boy to recite the "Hear, O Israel" prayer every evening leading up to the *bris*. In return, the children received a few hazelnuts and, on the night before the circumcision, honey-cakes that were as small as old-fashioned square coins. It was also the assistant's duty to make fringes for the *tsitsis* and *tales-kotn* worn by the children of the well-to-do householders who studied with his employer, and to purify in flowing water the new dishes of their wives.

The circumcision of my father's youngest son—Mordkhe

When my mother was forty-some years old, I remember her giving birth to my brother Mordkhe. Only five of her fourteen children had survived, and my brother Mordkhe was now the sixth. Father was over-joyed. Although my father was a little tight-fisted, in order to celebrate the birth of his son he prepared several kegs of beer, sieves filled with salted and peppered peas, many trays with onion cakes, and even several roasted chickens. And he did not have to announce that his doors were wide open to everyone in honor of the *bris*. The assistant brought tables and benches from all the synagogues. My father and I were the *kvaters*, the ceremonial godparents. I was five years old then. Father loved me very much and from then on used to call after me: "*Kvaterin*, where are you?"

The "Reshenke"

I still remember the beautiful, round crumb cake, the *reshenke* it was called, that father ordered from a sugar-baker. The *reshenke* was made in a special round copper basin that was as big as the bottom of a thousand-liter cask. The sugar coating was perfectly symmetrical and flat and was designed with a garland of flowers of large raisins and almonds. In the middle of the *reshenke*, they had spelled out *mazltov* in raisins and almonds, and sprinkled it all with gold leaf. After my brother had been "made a Jew," father cried out to me happily: "*Kvaterin* Hindze, come and take a big piece of this *reshenke*!"

My beloved son Zekharie, my beloved son Herts, my dear grand-daughter Blime-Ruth, my dear grandson Yosele—I hope you are not bored with my foolish stories of childhood. I am already sixty-seven years old and my memory doesn't always work properly. I am telling you simple things from years ago, moments that I can recall and also episodes from my school years. Perhaps it will be of interest to you one day.

The melamed from Sonik

I had another teacher whom we called the "Ne'er Do Well *melamed* from Sonik." Whenever someone wanted to hire the teacher, confusion ensued. "Where does this teacher live, this *melamed* from Sonik?" Nobody even knew his real name. The teacher from Sonik was in his thirties. He had a pale face, long, dark side curls, a shaved head, and a beard so sparse that you could count its hairs. His cheeks were hollow. He had no children. His wife sewed linens. His room was larger than those rooms in which I had studied with my earlier teachers but he had fewer students. Children did not want to study with him. Nevertheless, he had pupils. His *kheyder* was on Russian Street. One of his students lived on the same street. His name was Berl Koyfshteyn. To this day, I still cannot understand how his parents submitted their own flesh and blood to such torment. Nevertheless, Berl Koyfshteyn became the hero of the Ne'er Do Well's *kheyder*.

A little package

The teacher lay the boy down on the table every day, tugged his shirt out of his pants, immersed his pointer in salt water, and whipped him so hard that to this day—whenever I recount this—I still have tears in my eyes. The teacher frequently gave him "the package," which means that he would lay him across the table, pull the boy's shirt out up to his throat, stuff filthy rags into it, tie his shirt stuffed with the rags around his neck so he would look like a hunchback, put the handle of a broom in his hands, sully his little white, beautiful, rosy cheeks with a piece of coal, and leave him standing there like that until evening without giving him food or drink.

We thought that Berl Koyfshteyn had done nothing wrong. He was not a rowdy boy and he bothered nobody. There was one possible reason—he was a little slow. And his parents were not very wealthy.

The *melamed* from Sonik used to whip girls too. On those occasions he would roll down the sleeve of his shirt to cover the palm of his hand. He would then hit the girls over on their backs, over their blouses. Never with his bare hand and never on exposed skin.

The rebetsin—the wife of the melamed from Sonik

The *melamed*'s wife, the *rebetsin* as we used to call her, kept the *kheyder* room tidy, fresh, and swept. The beds were covered with white linen. Embroidered white edges were tucked into the bed frame. She too was well put together. Over her shaved head she wore a beautiful white bonnet made of linen. On the front of the cap there was an embroidered flounce, which was raised like a crown. There were bands of linen on both sides of the cap that hung down and were tied low around her throat like a butterfly. Her pale, white face was pretty enough, accented by her black eyebrows and eyelashes. Although her nose was a little wide, it was very charming. Her eyes were amber-yellow and her mouth was appealing.

The *rebetsin* taught the girls how to sew. She also would tell us many stories about Jewish holy men, *khasidic rebbes*, and great scholars. These had a great impact upon me. I was always thinking about piety. I would sit for the entire day in *kheyder*, and during the winter evenings I would even study the Bible. I dreamed of becoming a heavenly creature with wings.

Moyshe-Reuven, an enlightened teacher's assistant

But the *melamed* from Sonik soon left Redim. A more enlightened teacher arrived in his place. He taught us how to write Yiddish. He used to provide a writing sample for us and we were then required to copy it. This teacher came with his own name, Moyshe-Reuven.

On *Khanike*, he gave each student a *dreydl* made of lead that he had taken from the metal seals on flour sacks in the warehouse. He cast them in a wooden mold. He also played *dreydl* with the children. His *dreydls* had four sides, engraved with the four letters: *Nun, Gimel, Heh, Shin*. He explained the letters to us: "*Nun—Nat* (Here), *Gimel—Gonev* (Thief), *Heh—hakt* (Break), *Shin—Shleser* (Locks)." If the *dreydl* fell on the g—good, you won. When it fell on the n—nothing; on the sh—shucks; and on the h—half. He also played dominoes with us. He carved them out of wood all on his own. He burned the dots onto them with a hot glowing wire. The dominoes were very symmetrical, made to look exactly like those one could buy in a store. When he played with us, he left his tiles visible for all to see, but he still managed to win more often than we did.

Mendele the melamed

In truth, Moyshe-Reuven wasn't officially a teacher. For one thing, he was unmarried and he was also still very young. He was the assistant to our teacher, Mendele the *melamed*. But at the same time, he was the one who taught us how to write Yiddish. So we, the children, took him to be the true authority, and we listened to him. For us, Mendele the *melamed* was a nobody. He was not dynamic. Whether or not we followed along in the prayer book when he pointed at a letter or word with his white, bone pointer, he always gave the same foolish smile. He had a silly appearance. He was a short and thin little man, with a little white face. The blond hair on his head was sparse. So were his beard and mustache, only they were blonder and sparser so that one hair could search out another on his pale face to no avail. Even his teeth were sparse. His side locks were very small. All his clothes were clean and already somewhat "Germanic" considering the period.

More about Moyshe-Reuven

Moyshe-Reuven was an affable type; he was kind even to Mendele. He had a beautiful, intelligent face with even more intelligent, beautiful, gray, good-natured eyes. He had a thick black head of hair, a face not yet overgrown, and small, black *peyes*. During the winter, he wore a jacket lined with fur and a red scarf around his neck. People still remember Moyshe-Reuven because he was an assistant teacher in Redim for many years, until he was he hired to work in the forest as a wood assessor. He became such a specialist in this that he became a timber merchant himself.

After Moyshe-Reuven, I had many more teachers.

A teacher from Lemberg

One of these teachers came to our home and introduced himself: "I am a teacher from Lemberg!" I still remember what a foolish impression those words made on me. "I am a teacher from Lemberg …" And, in fact, he knew little more than how to introduce himself. But I studied with him. He would dictate stories from "A Thousand and One Nights" and from the *Mayse bukh* to the children.

Alfred Akselrod—a teacher from Stri

One of my teachers from the city of Stri, Alfred Akselrod, was even more progressive. He used to come to my house to teach me and three of my girlfriends in the little children's room. He taught us German and Yiddish. I still remember which books we read with him. The first was *Robinson Crusoe*. I remember how one of my girlfriends used to misread "*kapital*" (capital) instead of "*kapitl*" (chapter). No matter what, she repeated the same mistake: "Capital." Later, I remember, he told us to buy a book, *The Rose from Sonino*, and a second book whose title I can no longer recall. We never received either book and I never read them. Our handsome young teacher was in love, and for some reason unbeknownst to us he had been driven from his home. He was always sighing, poor thing, and he adorned our notebooks with German inscriptions that read: "Pani Akfan, why are you so distant from me?"

Whenever he went away for a few days, he would return paler, sadder, and more introverted. One of his students made fun of his sorrow and, looking at his drawn face, broke into loud laughter without any rhyme or reason. The teacher, poor thing, did not seem to notice and did not react.

Ignats Birn, a teacher from Yerslev

After the teacher from Stri, we had Ignats Birn from Yerslev. This teacher was already a "total Gentile," who also taught in the Polish school. I and my brother Neta went to his house to study. He lived with one of Father's uncles, Yoyne Bergner. He was a very good teacher and we learned something from every one of his classes. He taught only German and Polish. His face bore no trace of Jewishness. He had a round face with a turned-up nose, a tuft of dark-blond hair, a rosy-white face full of freckles, blue eyes with glasses, a well-developed body, and broad shoulders. He was certainly heavy enough for his age. Aunt Dvoyrtshe Bergner would prepare a breakfast according to his wishes that consisted of eight soft-boiled eggs and four large rolls smeared with a lot of butter. Having eaten such a breakfast, he would set out across the two big rooms with the shiny, polished floors and dance a mazurka or a krakoviak, lively Polish dances. He always poked fun at the way his sister spoke German: "*tish-tash, shpigl-shpogl, benkl-bankl.*"

The old pear tree

A few months later, another student joined us—my sister Mirl's son Mordkhe from Mikhalovke. He was a good-for-nothing. During that period, the teacher Birn came to our house to teach us. Whenever he arrived, my nephew Mordkhe was nowhere to be found. Most of the time, he was in the neighbor's pear tree, and I had to drag him to class. Mordkhe's behavior did not surprise me, because that old and sturdy pear tree drew me and all the neighbors' children to it like a magnet. We were enchanted by its small, fragrant pears. They were so beautiful to look at. When they were ripe and fell from the tree, they looked as though they had been painted by an artist—totally yellow with pinkish skin. In the season when fruit began to ripen, the tree really put up with a lot from us, especially from the boys. It is still there today—but it now looks like a hunched-over old man. Nor are its little pears the same anymore. Who knows—perhaps it is because I am old already and no longer gathering them in secret ... Its branches used to hang over our side of the fence. Just this year our former neighbor brought me some of its pears to taste.

I remember how much pleasure I derived whenever I managed to gather a whole box of ripe pears in the early dawn, or sometimes in a downpour when nobody else was around—ripe pears that had fallen because of the rain or the wind, the biggest and most beautiful. I would tease my girlfriends with its booty. That was sixty years ago. I am old now, and so is the pear tree. Children still throw stones at it, and it still brings forth fruit.

Ignats Birn converts

Now let us return to my nephew Mordkhe. Whenever he actually attended a class with Birn, he learned quite a lot. Mordkhe had a good mind, and Birn was a capable pedagogue. The teacher suddenly left Redim for the city of Kamionka-Strumilowa. Whether he was forced out or whether he chose to leave because he had converted and was too ashamed to be near his home in Yerslev, I don't know. My brother Neta regularly corresponded with the teacher in Kamionka-Strumilowa. As a result, my parents suspected that he too might convert. Neta was reading Schiller at the time. My parents destroyed the books and screamed at him: "You think you can keep this heretical filth in our home, you *sheygets,* you little *goy!*" But secretly, out of sight of our parents, he managed to study the classics of German literature.

My brother Neta's battle for European clothing

When my brother Neta became engaged, he still wore a *kolpak*, a traditional high fur hat, to prayer on the Sabbath. When he went to visit his bride in Yerslev, she naturally wanted him to dress in more contemporary European fashion. Father shouted at him and asked why he was wearing his pants over his boots (these were called "pantaloons"), and not tucking them into his boots. Within one week, he was already sporting a beaver hat and a long topcoat.

I remember a story about something my brother Neta did to Father. Several years after the wedding, my brother wanted Father to make him a sable pelt. He sent emissaries to Father, he begged Father, but all for naught. Suddenly, my brother had an idea. Father had always wanted him to dress piously, even to wear the *khasidic* fur-edged hat, the *shtrayml*, to the synagogue. So he shows up wearing a top hat one Sabbath, and peeks into the synagogue where my father is praying. Children, don't ask me how that stunt reverberated through Redim. First, Father became as pale as the wall, then red, then all the colors in between. "He has shamed me!" Father said, "He has become a modern—a German!"

My youngest brother—Mordkhe

My youngest brother Mordkhe was the *benzkunim*, the child of our parents' old age. Mother gave birth to him when she was already quite old. She had a difficult pregnancy and difficulty in childbirth. Both Father and Mother pampered him. I used to sleep in the same bed as my mother. I remember one summer evening when the midwife Sheyndl made up the bed and spread a colored slip under Mother's body. I protested and wanted to throw the slip away but Sheyndl, the old midwife, argued with me. I cried and protested loudly that I didn't want such a rag in my bed. My sister Laytshe, who was ten years older than I, enticed me away by promising to buy me soda water with lemon juice. That is how they got me out of the bed. And the very next day, the midwife presented me with my new little brother.

A four-piece coin in exchange for a fillip under the nose

My brother Mordkhe really loved money. Father used to play with him and agree to give him a four-piece coin in exchange for allowing him to give Mordkhe a fillip under the nose. Father used to play like that for several hours without my brother getting tired. His nose was red as a beet because of all the fillips. But Mordkhe wanted more and more coins. And I need not tell you that when he was not feeling well and was in bed, Father would sit next to him on the bed and cover an entire blanket with four-piecers in exchange for fillips. Father would tremble with laughter and pleasure.

My brother Mordkhe's private language

My youngest brother Mordkhe also invented his own language. He would add the letter *lamed* (an L-sound) to the end of every word. The cook's name was Blume—so he called her Blimerl. When she put bread in the oven, he said to her: "Blimerl, Blimerl, flatten the bread and park yourself down." And to the Jewish housekeeper, he used to say: "Her-sherl, you have a beardl and you are a pigl" … or "Fatherl, buy me a pakrl." A "pak" was a type of sugary fig on a stick. He called his mother "Meymeshi." I remember once, when Mother brought him one of the "fifteen fruits" on *Tu B'shvat*, he kissed and hugged her saying: "Meymeshi, Meymeshi, when you go shopping, do they give you a date'rl as a bonus?"

My brother Mordkhe studied in Mikhalovke. Our sister Mirl hired a teacher for her many sons. He did not wear a fur hat and Father did not react to his pants worn over his boots—pantaloons. When Mord-khe became engaged, he asked me to write love letters for him to his bride in Polish.

My brother Mordkhe's self-mortification

My brother Mordkhe reported for the draft four times (later, people were conscripted only three times). Every year before the mobilization he suffered along with all the other Jewish draftees by staying awake for nights on end. And during the day he took no rest but rather day-dreamed at the table with his head resting in his hand. Once he was daydreaming with his friend, also a draftee, in the children's room. I was already in bed but not yet asleep when I heard my brother's friend say: "I will write you a prescription that I've already tested on myself.

Take a book to read and you'll forget about sleep." Another time, before showing up before the draft board, my brother got himself drunk so that in the morning, when he appeared, he would look terrible. He came over to my house crying and screaming, "It's a shame that I studied Abaye and Rava for eighteen years," while he struck his head with his fists. My son Moyshe was three at the time. Seeing his uncle drunk, he began to cry and ask: "*Wujciu, nie placz, bo politcja cię wezmie do aresztu*" (Uncle, don't cry because the police will come and arrest you). And Zekharie, then only one-and-a-half years old, you were also afraid that Uncle Mordkhe would be arrested. The next day, my brother Mordkhe appeared before the conscription board in Yerslev. When he was exempted from duty, he telegraphed home the following words: "*zohn khofshi*" (son free). I was overjoyed. To make amends for the fuss and panic he had sown in the children, my brother bought me a big plush carpet to put underneath the table.

I also remember how Father once played a joke on Mordkhe. When my brother was already engaged, he gave Mordkhe a fifty to hold onto and asked him: "So you like money, do you?" My brother pretended that he didn't understand and he didn't want to give back the fifty. It was fifty Gulden.

Yes, my brother Mordkhe really loved money. And as the youngest of my parents' sons, he was given a dowry of five thousand Rheinisch. His bride received a dowry of eight thousand Rheinisch, which, back then, amounted to sixteen thousand Crowns. When World War I broke out, my brother was already worth fifty thousand Austrian Crowns. He has three daughters. Two live in Switzerland. One daughter is a doctor in a hospital in Basel; the other is a pharmacist in Zurich. He gave every last cent of his inheritance from Father to his two daughters, who were studying abroad in Switzerland. Today they want nothing to do with their father.

His wife and youngest daughter never let him out of their sight. If he came home without pockets full of money, or less than five kilograms of sugar, they—his own wife and daughter—would push him out the door again into the corridor in the dark of night and shout at him in Polish: "If you come home without any money or any sugar, get lost!" And more than once, poor Mordkhe—this indulged youngest son of rich parents—was forced to spend the night in the corridor. Sometimes the wife and daughter threw him out, winter or summer, wearing only his underwear. For years he wandered around the Yerslev railway station. On many occasions, he ran away and arrived on foot at my place in Redim. Usually, he arrived on a Friday night, all bloodied, with only rags on his feet. Your father was stunned the first time this happened. Later, we became accustomed to his visits.

Once, when he had been staying with us for quite some time, my sister-in-law Sabine arrived with her Polish servant. Sabine stood guard over my room, which had a separate entrance. When Mordkhe found out that "Madame" was there, he locked himself in the room. His wife Sabine stood by the window on the veranda. Her servant— a Hercules—waited by the door. And that is where they remained an entire winter's night. Before daylight, the servant—a tall and hefty Gentile—knocked the door off its hinges, and tied a rope around both of my brother's hands. With the encouragement of his wife, my brother finally allowed himself be led to the train like a circus bear. He did not seem ashamed and he let himself be led away quietly. It was still dark, but a lot of people witnessed the scene. And they told your father and me about it!

Your father couldn't stand Sabine. Once, when my brother was staying with us again for an extended period, he saw his wife arriving in the distance. He picked himself up and fled to Ostrov. Sabine believed that he was still in our house. She stationed herself by the door. Your father could not tolerate the scene of a woman tormenting a man, and he was furious with her. He opened the door and said to her: "Where is your servant with the rope? Mordkhe is under the bed and has to be dragged out." Oh, it was so funny to watch my sister-in-law, her hat on her head, rolling around under the beds looking for her husband! Unable to find him, she refused to believe that he was not in our house. She harassed us until late into the night. The police had to be called to force her to leave. Yet Mordkhe gave in to her more and more.

It took many years of adventures and scandals until my brother at last came to his senses and finally stood up to her. When his wife and daughter pulled his hat off his head in the middle of the street in Yerslev, he pulled off his daughter's glasses. Another time he crept into the house when his wife and daughter were not home, gathered up all his belongings, and left for good. Since that time, he has rented a small apartment for himself and become a man like all other men, earning a living and dressing respectably. Before, when he was still with his wife, he went around in rags like a madman. Now everyone who looks at him thinks he must have won the lottery.

My sister Laytshe's first marriage

My sister Laytshe died in 1935 at the age of seventy-five. She was married at seventeen. I remember her wedding as if it were a dream. After the ceremony, when people were already preparing to partake of the wedding feast, the master of ceremonies rode in on a horse while singing a Polish song. I was so frightened that I fell off the bench I was standing on.

Shloyme-Zalmen, my brother-in-law, who died young

My sister Laytshe's first husband was Shloyme-Zalmen. He truly was a handsome man. He had curly, chestnut-brown hair, a beautiful Greek nose, and laughing brown eyes. All in all, he was a pale brunette, and very well put together. My father adored him. Shloyme-Zalmen managed Father's books and assisted him in the grain trade. Once, he traveled with my sister Laytshe, his wife, to Mikhalovke over the Sabbath of *Khanike*. Sunday, when they returned home healthy and refreshed, a cobbler brought him new boots. But the boots were too narrow for him and he couldn't get them off. He struggled with them so hard that he fell ill on the spot. Two doctors were brought from Yerslev but they could not help. He died a few days later at the tender age of twenty-two. He left behind a one-and-a-half-year-old daughter—Rivtshe.

My father mourns Shloyme-Zalmen

My father could not forget his beloved son-in-law. I often found my father sobbing inconsolably in the attic with the writings that Shloyme-Zalmen had left behind. Out of curiosity, I used to go over to the wicker basket and look at these writings penned in blue ink. The letters were round and small like fine, round pearls. I could not understand what he had written. An entire basket of such beautiful paper, filled with blue ink. Beautiful and bundled together, but with the ink a little smudged because of my father's tears. Rivtshe, his daughter, still visits the grave of the father she never knew.

I too loved my brother-in-law. He used to joke with me and teach me various riddles. I already knew how to write a little Yiddish when my handsome, kind brother-in-law became so gravely ill. I wrote on all the tables and benches in chalk: "May he live." During his entire illness, I pleaded with God to return him to good health. It took me a long time to get him out of my mind. To this day, I don't understand why my sister Laytshe mourned him so little.

Rivtshe, Shloyme-Zalmen's daughter

Their daughter Rivtshe was one and a half years old when he died. She had had a twin sister. Even though the other girl was raised at home and had a very good wet-nurse, she died after only four weeks. Rivtshe was given to Freydele the wig mender, a very poor local woman. My sister Laytshe had a very difficult time during labor and for many years she hovered between life and death. When Rivtshe finally was brought home from that woman, she was miserable because she had been neglected. A good, healthy wet-nurse was hired for her. Rozye was her name. Father would not allow her to be fired. Rozye nursed Rivtshe until she was five years old.

Rivtshe was often sick with intestinal parasites, and when she had a fever, she could be a real nag and yell: "*Ròziu, spiewaj ptaszek* (Rozye, sing bird)." Father used to stand by her crib for nights on end. And when she was healthy again, he would mimic her: "*Ròziu, spiewaj ptaszek.*" When, after five years, the wet-nurse left for Yerslev, Rivtshe longed for her and so did I. I went with Rivtshe to visit her nurse in Yerslev, where she was already employed in the home of a judge.

My sister Laytshe, your aunt, regularly ate her meals at Grandfather's table. My father treated Rivtshe, her daughter, better than his own children, all because of his compassion for her being left an orphan so young.

Laytshe with pockets full of newspaper

Laytshe's second husband, Hirsh-Volf, was a bachelor. You knew him, children. Laytshe used to wear a pinafore with two deep pockets. The pockets were always stuffed full of newspapers. The first paper was the *Wiener Israelit*, a German-Jewish newspaper from Vienna. Later, Royze-Mindl, the dressmaker, who had family in America, supplied her with stacks of Yiddish newspapers. Royze-Mindl referred to them as "tales of Jewish romance." My sister was interested in all of them. She also used to speak fondly about her teachers, and about how years ago private teachers provided a better education than today's schools. Laytshe had very beautiful Yiddish calligraphy, perfectly round handwriting. She also wrote Polish and German well. She used to talk about one teacher who was known as "the vulgar teacher" because when somebody said to him "it's on the tip of my tongue," he would answer "take it off and speak faster."

After Mother's death, all the grandchildren, including you, my children, used to call out to Laytshe: "*Babcia Laytshia, daj nam shabes-oybst*" (Grandma Laytshe, give us Sabbath fruit).

Avrom-Moyshe, Laytshe's miracle child from the Komarne Rebbe

Laytshe did not have children with her husband Hirsh-Volf for ten years. As soon as the old *rebbe* from Komarn—a relative of Uncle Leybush—arrived, my sister Laytshe went with her husband to the *rebbe* with a *kvitl*, a type of supplicatory note, and a *pidyen*, a sum to secure its efficacy. The *rebbe* asked for money. I no longer recall precisely how much. And soon after, she gave birth to a son, Avrom-Moyshe. Don't laugh! The Komarne *Rebbe* regularly asked for a larger sum from women who did not yet have children. One woman could not have children for eighteen years and then the *rebbe* performed a real miracle for her. He distributed all the money he collected to the needy. Or at least that is what I remember people saying about him.

Avrom-Moyshe becomes a student

Of course the miracle child courtesy of the Rebbe, Avrom-Moyshe, was sent off for a secular education. It is impossible to describe the upheaval this caused in town. How could it be—Laytshe's son, a "student?" He studied in Yerslev in the secular high school. When he came home, he changed out of his student uniform and pulled his side locks forward. But when he returned to school, he would hide those same curls behind his ears. People would call after him:

> *Student, student*
> *Halt di hoyzn in di hent*
> (Keep your pants from falling down)

It was nice when he came home, put on the long coat and the velvet hat, and let his two straight side curls hang down, but it really wasn't him. It lasted only until graduation.

Laytshe's children

My sister Laytshe gave birth to three children fathered by Hirsh-Volf, two sons and one daughter. The Komarne *Rebbe*'s miracle child, Avrom-Moyshe, is an engineer, now fifty years old. Her second son, Itsik, is a lawyer. He is very capable and could have been the second Leyb Landoy. But he strayed from the "straight and narrow," and lost everything.

Laytshe "bought" a medical doctor for her daughter Etl, but my sister did not derive much pride from her either. Etl's husband left her for the Soviet Union, and she was barely able to get him to agree to give her a divorce before he took off.

She was proudest of her oldest daughter Rivtshe, the child of her first husband, Shloyme Zalmen. A few years before her death, Laytshe left her entire estate to Rivtshe with the provision that she support her mother in her sickness, provide her with a decent burial, give a few hundred zlotys to charity, and have her son-in-law Yeshaye recite the *kadish* in her memory. She saw to all this years before her death. Laytshe remained in control of her faculties until the day she died in her sleep.

Rivtshe's children

Rivtshe, the survivor of twins, bore nine children, three daughters, five sons, and one baby who suffocated on the breast of the wet-nurse who was sleeping with her. Her oldest daughter, Dortshe, is very attractive. She, like her grandfather Shloyme Zalmen, is very good-natured. She married a cousin from her father's side of the family and lives in Budapest. Her husband is also a kind, intelligent, good man. He is financially quite comfortable, but they do not have any children. As a result, both Dortshe and her husband adore her youngest brother Manele Lev, so much so that they want to adopt him. Rivtshe's three sons are already married. They live in Warsaw. They are all gifted and intelligent. The oldest is Shloyme, the middle one is Melekh. He had a boorish peasant for a wet-nurse. Rivtshe complained that he took after his wet-nurse with his "coarse manners." Rivtshe's third son, Nakhum, is an engineer. He fell in love with a girl from Warsaw when he was quite young. Of course, neither had money, but they married anyhow.

The story with Nakhum Lev goes like this. Melekh Lev had already been in Warsaw a long time and he certainly knew a lot of girls. Once, when he came home to 90 Mickiewicz Street in Pshemishl, one of these girls followed him and stayed with Etl Gutt, who lived just across from the Levs. But the girl's more attractive sister also came to visit and stayed with Etl. Nakhum, who was a handsome and tall young bachelor, had only just finished his first year of technical studies, but he quickly fell in love with this girl. I was in Pshemishl at the time when the Warsaw girls were living with Etl. Rivtshe complained to me that the money Dortshe had sent to support Nakhum in his studies (and also some extra for a vacation) was wasted by Nakhum on the girls. Soon after that, Itsik Gutt's son, Babush, dropped by to inform us that Nakhum had taken the prettier girl—or she had taken him—and together they had run away to Warsaw to get married. Nakhum wanted Rivtshe to go with him to attend the ceremony, but she refused because she did not approve of the marriage. But as soon as he was gone she regretted her decision. She picked herself up and went after them. She thought that she could stop him, at least until he finished his studies. But she didn't stand a chance. He had already put on a suit and a top hat, and was standing under the wedding canopy. And Dortshe had to send him money to finish his studies.

Rivtshe has only one grandchild, Nakhum's little daughter. Her two daughters, Etl and Blimke, are not yet married.

Yeshaye Lev lent his daughter Dortshe—or should we say his son-in-law—ten thousand zlotys. But for several years now, that way of "earning" a living has disappeared. People don't trust anyone anymore, and prefer to keep their money under the mattress. But their children are earning a living. Berte earns about 250 zlotys a month, and Nosn, who still lives at home and is not yet married, earns 150 zlotys. And Dortshe sends as much as she can from Hungary, because that is now the accepted practice.

For two years now, since 1935, Rivtshe has been living in Pshemishl. Her mother, Laytshe, died, and she does not get along well with the Gutt family. They are constantly hauling one another into court. It is more comfortable for her to live in town, because it is closer for the children to get to work. And it is frightening to go out at night nowadays. The Levs live at Smolki Street, number 7. And for two years now, Rivtshe has provided room and board for a student for 50 zlotys a month.

I shall chatter on and later, when I have more patience, I will try to tell you something about your father's side of the family, and then a little about the life your father and I shared. I doubt I shall succeed. But so long as my eyes remain open and my mind serves me well, I will write. What will be will be. You, my children, will have this to remember me by. At least that's how I imagine it. I would have liked to live several more years with your father so that we could have derived pride together in your writing.

More about several matches

I return now to several matches that were proposed to me. One was with Leon from Tarne, a very handsome man. I even fancied him a bit. But nobody asked me. And since he was already self-sufficient, he did not want to remain in Redim supported by his father-in-law. So nothing happened, and there was no match.

Another self-sufficient prospect called "Kokok" was tall, broad, and not particularly handsome. He had a sickly face. I could not even bear it when he talked to me.

The proposals were quite annoying. But my parents succeeded in persuading me that, at the age of only sixteen, I was an old maid.

The match with your father

One time, a relative of your father from Sambor, Dvoyre Bergner, sent a postcard proposing her cousin Efrayim from Stanislavov. Here is how I found out about it—by reading the card that was lying on the big desk. I also heard my brother Neta tell his friend about a boy from Stanislavov, Efrayim Bergner, who had presented himself to the draft in Yerslev, but had been dismissed from the fourth class. While talking about him, he pointed: "That's him returning from the post office." Hearing this I ran to our alcove window to look at him. He appealed to me. Black, curly hair, black eyes, and olive skin. But I did not reveal this to anyone.

Soon after your father arrived in Redim, Uncle Itshl Katz from Sosnitse proposed the same match. We were finally brought together to meet in Lemberg.

[At this point in the memoirs, the manuscript is missing several pages dealing with the description of Hinde and Efrayim's first meeting and the terms of their engagement.]

My bridegroom comes for a visit

If I remember correctly, your father came to visit as a bridegroom on a Tuesday in July. He brought me a gold bracelet set with diamonds, and gave me an elegant travel kit containing manicure instruments that were quite rare in those days. I enjoyed that gift more than the gold and diamonds.

After consulting with the older children, Father sent my fiancé and me to Mikhalovke for the Sabbath. I did not argue; on the contrary, I was very happy. But my fiance could not understand why they were sending him, an honored guest, away. Did they think that he would not be able to recite the blessing properly if he was called up to the Torah? However, I understood my father and I knew that he hated a commotion. He was thanking God that he had somewhere to send us. He informed Mikhalovke about the plan and a nice carriage was sent for us with a pair of beautiful fast horses. It was a delightful, warm July day and we were off to Mikhalovke, to the earthly Garden of Eden. No longer bound up in our urban home in Redim, we were free to roam about in the open air. Nobody was curiously observing us, except for the servants.

We went to bathe, your father with our nephew Khayim, and I with our young niece Frimtshe. It was a Friday. On the Sabbath before noon, a prayer quorum of several neighbors from the countryside gathered inside. Your father recited the blessing in a resounding voice without making a single mistake. Father would have been very proud of my groom, but now it was too late. Yes, I forgot to tell you that on Friday night when your father was holding the goblet during the *kidesh*, his hand was shaking so much that people must have thought he was afraid of something. I was a little embarrassed that I had a fiancé whose hands shook in front of these people.

The Sabbath stroll of the bride and groom

On the Sabbath, after we had finished the meal, we went for a walk, first in the big orchard where we gathered pears and apples that had fallen because of the wind, and later in an Eden-like garden of blackberries, strawberries, currants, and white and red gooseberries. The gooseberry and currant shrubs spread over the entire length of the garden. Several fruit trees also grew in the garden: trees with pearmain apples, oily *funtvoke* apples, great juicy pears, two greengage trees with a type of plum that made your mouth water. Even grapes were growing there. We also found all kinds of vegetables and flowers: red, pink, and yellow roses, red and yellow raspberries for jam, entire trees with little roses, and two great fir trees. In the midst of it all there was a gazebo with benches that was encircled by trees so that one could enjoy both sun and shade in the garden. And we walked through all this gloriousness arm in arm. Your father, my fiancé, protected me from the sun with his hat because it would have been a sin to carry a parasol on the Sabbath.

We were escorted back to Redim Saturday night by our nephew Khayim Dim. My father was really pleased with us. He was happy that he had not had to rush around that Sabbath. He asked us whether we had eaten the big oily apples, the "*funtvokes*," which cost him a hundred apiece. That is how he hinted to us that he was losing money from our estate in Mikhalovke.

Efrayim Bergner, Stanislavov 1890

The wedding gathering in Khirov

Even my father escaped to Khirov for my wedding. There were two inns by the train station in Khirov, one next to the other. My family stayed in one hotel, and my groom's family stayed in the other.

My wedding gifts

I was given several wedding gifts right away: a wig and an elegant white felt hat with genuine, long, white ostrich feathers. Between the feathers, you could make out a tiny, little green bird. The feathers were stitched diagonally across the hat, one over the other, and hung down at the back of my neck, ending in a plush little ribbon. The hat was similar in shape to a hunter's cap. I also received a white prayer book bound in white ivory, ornamented in gold, a golden locket, and a white cape made of plush brocade. It suited the delicate white silk of my wedding gown. The cape was adorned with white fur at the neck. I wore the cape underneath the wedding canopy. I was very pleased with my bridal veil and the fresh myrtle garland that resembled a crown. But your father was not pleased with the garland, and he told me after the wedding ceremony that when he realized what had happened to it, he bit his lips in annoyance. All his efforts to make the garland look like a real crown were for nothing and, to top it off, it was put over my veil backward. The bouquet of roses was also beautiful. The white roses were fresh. Every flower was bound below with wire, and set into a pretty muslin cuff. They were arranged from above with pleated muslin lace and tiny white tassels stuck into them. The bouquet was made to complement the wedding gown. A delicate, white satin ribbon, almost a meter in length, hung down from the bouquet.

Guests from the groom's side

The wedding was held in the month of *Kheshvn,* in the autumn of 1891. I fasted, and before I was led to the wedding canopy, I prayed with great intensity. I don't remember whether I cried underneath the wedding canopy. At the wedding, there were many relatives from your father's side of the family: Aunt Dvoyre Bergner with her husband Khone and their son Nekhemie. Aunt Dvoyrtshe had been the principal matchmaker. Their son Nekhemie, who was not yet married but was already self-sufficient, was an official at the steam mill in Pshemish. It was rumored that he was very stingy and not very nice. He looked after everything himself, he cooked for himself, he darned his own socks. He made a handsome living, but did not care to share a cent with his siblings. He would say: "My sister and brothers ought to earn their own money." He left for Hungary to serve as director of a large mill. He married in Hungary and continues to live there. He watched me the entire ceremony and later told me that I seemed very serious.

There was a *badkhn,* a traditional wedding entertainer, from Pshemishl at the wedding who was more intelligent than most wedding jesters of the period, really more poet than jester. I think that his name was Landau. Your father's sister Khane, her husband Ziskind Kris, and their three children—two daughters and a son—came from Vienna especially for the wedding. Your father's other siblings also came: Yeshaye Katz no. 1, Aunt Reyzl's husband, and Yeshaye Katz no. 2, Aunt Khave's husband. Your Uncle Zekharie came with his wife Tsivtshe, and Uncle Akive came by himself. Uncle Meshulem was left behind at home with the servants, which really upset your grandfather, who was inclined to order him to come on the very next express train. Your great-grandfather Yitskhok Bergner, his sons, his grandsons and his great-grandsons came from Sambor, as did one of his sons from Tismienitse with his grandsons.

Guests from the bride's side

From my side of the family, there was Father, Mother, my sister Mirl with her husband Avrom-Hirsh, my parents' oldest son-in-law. Laytshe and her husband Hirsh-Volf stayed behind to watch over the house. Aunt Laytshe was pregnant at the time with Itsik. Of my brothers, Noyekh was there without his wife, and Note was also there without his wife because Aunt Hindze was pregnant with Salke. My Uncle Dovid Mayster and Aunt Khaye-Sore were there, as were Aunt Hendl from Siftshene and Uncle Hirsh-Volf's two sisters from Pshemish. Yes, it is good that I remembered to include Aunt Sime Berglos with her husband Yosl Berglos and their daughter Hinde-Reyzl from Redim. Uncle Itshl Katz from Sosnitse, our second matchmaker, and my cousin Sore Shtern from Yerslev also attended.

Dovid 'Bogacz', the waiter from Redim

For a long time after the wedding your father could not forget that after the ceremony, when people already had sat down to eat, the waiter whom we had brought with us from Redim approached him.

He was a fat, ruddy, middle-aged, freckled little Jew with a broad, flat nose. He was known as Dovid "Bogacz" (Polish for "a wealthy man"), but his real name was David Shvartsshteyn. He used to strut around with a gold medal pinned to his jacket. He was very proud of that medal. He boasted that when he had returned from the front, he suddenly found himself a rich man—a *bogacz*—and that is how he took on the last name. The brown, padded coat that he wore looked as though he had slaughtered with his own hands the roasted geese that he brought with him to serve to our guests. Both corners of his coat were turned up and tucked into his belt. He came to the wedding table with a big basin and a jug of water in his hands. He shoved them before your father, the groom, and barked: "Here, groom, wash!" For a long time after, your father could not get over how he had been shamed by this small town ignoramus we had brought with us to serve such noble, intelligent relatives.

Your father's grandfather, Reb Yitskhok

My dear sons and grandchildren, before I begin to tell you about how your father's grandfather, Reb Yitskhok Bergner from Sambor, rejoiced at his grandson's wedding, I will first describe him for you the same way your father, who was familiar with his lineage and intelligence, once did for me. Your great-grandfather Reb Yitskhok Bergner truly deserved the honorific "Reb" because he was a descendant of great rabbinic minds. He was a close relative of Rabbi Meshulem Landoy from the district of Tismienitse. Reb Yitskhok was the type of scholar who sat day and night studying Torah. I think that he also wrote several books in Hebrew. He owned a big library with all kinds of books, mainly by German writers. He was very inspired by Heine, whose lines from the poem "Disputation" he used to recite by heart: "*Daß der Rabbi und der Mönch, Daß sie alle beide …*" Because of his opinions and the nature of the books he studied, he often concealed what he was doing by retreating to the study space he organized for himself in the attic, the one with a secret entry.

When your father and I met Reb Yitskhok after our wedding at Uncle Kalmen Bergner's in Tismienitse for the engagement of one of his grandsons, he told us that he once was caught with a German book and only barely escaped excommunication.

Reb Yitskhok's dance with all the children and children's children

Now I will return to tell you about how, after our wedding feast, Reb Yitskhok Bergner gathered all the relatives in a big, clean, elegant, dance hall in another hotel. He brought together his entire family—sons, daughters, grandchildren, great-grandchildren. Then he called us in, the bride and groom. He arranged the entire family in a big circle and beamed with joy and pride.

Reb Yitskhok was a handsome Jew of medium height. He was already gray. He had delicate features, friendly gray eyes, thick, curly gray hair and a well-manicured gray beard. His side curls were so cleverly inconspicuous that they were almost unnoticeable. A white, beautifully pressed, wide collar peeked out from under his shirt in the "Slowacki" style. On his handsome, elegant head sat a black velvet *yarmulke* that looked as if it had grown directly out of his black, curly hair. Underneath his unbuttoned silk coat, which had a slit in the back like a fitted dressing gown, he wore a beautifully embroidered black velvet vest. His trousers were made of dark fabric. They were wide and tucked into his clean, cotton-white, handmade, knit socks. They looked like the knickers of today. The socks were fastened with silk ribbons. On his feet he wore glossy black slippers that passed for dancing shoes.

The dance that Reb Yitskhok asked the *klezmer* band to play was called a "*sher*," a lively Jewish dance. At the beginning, we all stood in a big circle with our hands locked together, circling a few times. After that, grandfather asked them to play a "*czardas*," a Hungarian dance that begins slowly but ends wildly. Grandfather went into the middle of the circle, dancing and singing and clapping his hands to the beat of the music. He grabbed my hand first and danced the "*czardas*" with me as if he were a young man. Then, he locked our hands—the groom's and mine. He placed his hand over ours, and he blessed us in several languages with a beautiful melody. We kissed him on the hand and he kissed us on our foreheads.

My father is not pleased with my husband's grandfather

My mother was very happy that she happened upon such fine, elegant people as her new in-laws. And she was also pleased that her youngest daughter—her third—had a husband already, and one with a Jewish heart to boot, because under the wedding canopy your father wore the *shtrayml* that had been sent to him. My father, in contrast, wanted to escape from everything quickly and return home as fast as possible. He could not comprehend the merry-making of grandfather Reb Yitskhok, and the huge party he had arranged for us. He could not understand how an old man could have had such an idea and how he made himself look so foolish and childish with all his dancing and singing. He let it be known that, in his opinion, the entire affair seemed a frivolous comedy. In the middle of the night, my father left the entire wedding celebration and took the first train home. He left money behind with his oldest grandson, Avrom-Hirsh, to pay for everything that we owed and also for anything else that the guests might order. He just wanted to be left in peace. "I can't take it any more. It's shameful … It's making me dizzy and I'm going home to drink my own tea. The tea at the wedding is already making my head heavy. And that strong horseradish is giving me heartburn …"

My father leaves the wedding and goes home

That is what Father said when he went home. Since I understood my father and his weak nerves, I did not hold it against him when he left my wedding early. I knew that he did not intend any harm, and that he wasn't trying to save any money by leaving. An entire night of dancing, frolicking, drinking, and smoking was beyond what he could stand. Home from the wedding, my poor father drew one of his Persian nightcaps over his ears and groaned the entire night. He was awake even the night after, pacing around the house and groaning. My father suffered from headaches for over fifty years. I will return later to tell you about how my father worried about the family's financial security, how careful he was to supervise the management of his businesses so that they would not fall apart. I will also tell you about his wonderful goodness and honesty.

The bouquet of white roses at the end of the wedding

Now I will recount another source of grief for your father at the wedding. After many of our relatives had departed because they had an early train connection to take them home, all of us from Redim began to gather for our train. Your father asked me where my bouquet was because he wanted to pack it up in the little box in which he had brought it from Stanislavov. The waiter, Dovid Bogacz, was already holding all the packages and luggage, including the expensive bouquet, in his hands. He could not have cared less that the bouquet was pressed, squeezed, and tied tightly with a white satin bow. All its white roses had been torn off. Bogacz told me that two stout young women, my cousins Sore Shtern and Hinde-Reyzl Berglas, had torn off the roses. I was angry with my cousin Sore and your father was even more furious with his cousin Hinde-Reyzl. Neither had any concern for his great effort and care in acquiring the bouquet. It required an effort in those days to come by such beautiful white roses during the cold months, and your father must have used his connections with Baron Romashkin. Poor thing, I went home empty-handed, without roses.

I keep my own hair

All of us from Redim caught the train from Khirov to Pshemishl. In Pshemishl, we disembarked and waited a few hours at the hotel "Pod Dębem" for the train to Redim. We had lunch at that hotel. The proprietor, a nosy Jewish woman who sported her natural hair, came into our room and removed the hat from my head so as to see whether my hair had been shorn. My mother was shamed and disgraced because of me. But your father did not remain silent, and in the end it was the hotel proprietor who left greatly ashamed.

Uncle Itshl Katz and the Bosnian knives

Uncle Itshl Katz, our matchmaker, was in our carriage on the way to Redim. There was also a Bosnian in the same car, carrying with him Bosnian knives. Uncle Itshl never ceased bargaining with him over the knives, and he actually bought several dozen from him. Although your father tried to dissuade him from buying the knives, he did not pay any attention to him and laughed. He said: "You will see, Froykele, how much I will earn from these knives, and also have a souvenir of your wedding."

We all laughed. I was unaware that he was far from a genius, and I took him quite seriously. He impressed me as a very good person. A few years after our wedding, he built a house with an extra large room so that he could lodge poor guests and host celebrations. But after our wedding fate was not kind to him. When he returned home with the Bosnian knives, his wife threw him out along with his newest purchase.

Going to synagogue on the Sabbath

And now I will tell you, my dear children, how I was led to synagogue on the Sabbath after my wedding. That Sabbath morning, Freydele the wig maker combed the two long braids on the wig she brought for me. I put the wig on over my own hair, which was already quite long. I did this for my mother's sake. She begged me with tears in her eyes to wear the wig at least the first time I went to synagogue as a married woman. She preached to me, explaining that your father, even though he was from Stanislavov, had worn a *shtrayml*. She lectured me about how I was acting smug and enlightened, and that I needed to keep in mind that your father was a pious Jew. Perhaps you can imagine how I looked, wearing that hunter's cap with the three long, large ostrich feathers over the wig and those long braids, all over my own hair. I wore a black silk dress with a train. Over it I sported a black plush coat with a Maria Stuart collar, adorned with shining feathers. At home, the ladies of our town gathered to lead me to the synagogue. When I finished applying my make-up, my mother placed a prayer book in my right hand and invited me, the bride, to take the first step. The women all cried out in one voice: "*Mit dem rekhtn fus, in a mazldiker sho*"(the best of luck, may you be off to a good start), a popular expression of good wishes.

I walked at the head of the procession with two other young wives, too embarrassed to look back at the crowd of women behind us. I did not pray because it is a custom to seat a new bride next to the rabbi's wife, and for the bride only to hold the prayer book in her hands, not to open it, so that if ever there were a bride who did not know how to pray, she would not be shamed in public.

Returning from synagogue—twenty-some 'kidushn'

After I returned home from synagogue, the women ran straight for the honey-cake, torte, liqueur, and preserves. I followed slowly after them. When the women left, an entire prayer house of men arrived with the groom. The groom wore a wide *shtrayml* with thirteen points and a sable fur that was also quite wide. But his *shtrayml* accidently had fourteen edges. It fell over your father's small head, almost down to his ears. Nevertheless, his little, black, sparkling, laughing eyes shone even more. After the *kidesh*, your father and I, escorted by my parents, paid visits to close relatives, acquaintances, and friends.

We returned home flushed from twenty-some glasses of *kidesh* wine, and bites of shtrudel, tort, and jam. Your father said that he enjoyed most of all the *esrog* jam with which Aunt Khaye Sore had honored us. She said that it was a holy jam, because Uncle Leybush had prayed in synagogue and recited *hallel* with that very *esrog*.

Sheve brokhes

After eating, the *sheve brokhes*, traditional benedictions delivered under the wedding canopy and for the week following the marriage, were recited and more guests arrived. People sent kugels, wine, beer, mead, and hazelnuts. This is still the custom with us today, though people are no longer as generous.

Saturday night, some Polish musicians from Sosnitse came to play for us. So did Uncle Itshl Katz with his wife and children, and my sister Mirl with her children from Mikhalovke. Sheyndl the midwife went out to invite all the girls in town. The merriment extended late into the night. During the festivities, people snacked on fine torts and refreshed themselves with cold soda water with raspberry syrup because back then we had not heard yet of ice cream. Throughout the celebration my father slept peacefully and nobody disturbed him because everything took place in two large rooms that had been especially emptied for the occasion. The doors and windows of the rooms faced out to the courtyard. All the noise went outside through the open windows and doors. And my father's precious sleep was protected.

By Sunday morning, everything was back in its proper place as if nothing had happened. My father was in Seventh Heaven because now the entire ordeal, thank God, was behind him.

Led to bed

I ought also to mention how "*kosher*" my wedding was. I immersed myself in the ritual bath a day before the ceremony. After the wedding canopy, the bride and groom were locked for a moment in a room together to mark the custom of *yikhud*, but really only for a moment. The door was soon opened. There is one thing I am quite embarrassed to recount to you, my children, but I will in any case because it was characteristic of that time. After all our guests who had a train connection late that night had departed, the close relatives spent the night in the hotel. And before I knew what was happening, my mother and mother-in-law led me to a room to go to bed, and they left me all alone.

But I soon noticed that I was not alone in the room. My groom was also there. Only then did I understood that those who had led me to the room had been guiding us to bed. I lay down fully clothed. I dared not undress. When my husband approached me, I felt an aversion to him, even though I had already met him three times before: once at the "inspection" in Lemberg, the next time at the engagement there, and the third time when he was invited to visit us in Redim. And although I liked my fiancé well enough, I suddenly felt repelled by him. Perhaps I was ashamed? The bridegroom crept closer to my bed and out of fear (I still remember that feeling well) I began to tremble. And I quickly turned toward the wall. My husband asked me why I was angry with him. I did not answer him. That is how things remained until morning. I think that I kept my eyes shut the entire time even though I did not sleep a wink. Only when I saw my husband fully clothed in the morning did I understand that people were preparing to go home. My husband asked me whether I had slept and he said that he was going to bring me my coat because it was time for the train. And only then did I begin to answer his questions and become a little friendlier.

Our wedding trip to Rzhabtsh

We already had our own apartment set up at home, though it really consisted of little more than a bedroom. We used to spend the entire day with my parents. I still remember the paintings on the headboard of our iron beds. There was a little picture of a loving couple who were floating in a little boat and plucking water flowers. For several days after the wedding, until we left for Rzhabtsh, my mother kept coming into our bedroom to check on something. And as your father tells it, she was angry with him because of his behavior toward me. That Friday we arrived in Rzhabtsh before candle-lighting and my sister-in-law was very upset. She had already lit candles and did not have any candlesticks for me. My brother-in-law, Motl Hitner, either pretended he did not understand or else he wanted to show us how liberal he was. He quickly extinguished the Sabbath candles that his wife had already blessed and gave me the candlesticks so that I could recite the blessing too. I looked at my sister-in-law with surprise, but I was too embarrassed to react to my brother-in-law's behavior, and so I recited the blessing over my sister-in-law's candlesticks.

A Belz Khosid who eats on a fast day

We went to Rzhabtsh, a village near Belz, for our honeymoon. We stayed for about two weeks. Every day, my brother-in-law Hitner took us in his carriage to a different town. The first day, we went to Belz. It was a fast day, the *Tenth of Tevet*. We went to my brother-in-law's friend, Nekhemie Vayninger, who ran a grocery store. One could buy supplies for an entire week there. We were invited to his home, whose windows faced out onto a street. It was noon. The family closed the curtains, began to set the table, and invited us to eat. Even Reb Nekhemie, who pretended to be a *khosid* from Belz, sat with us and ate.

I was flabbergasted that such a thing could take place in a city where *rebbe*s had lived for generations. A Jew like Reb Nekhemie Vayninger was not fasting?!

To top it all, Nekhemie Vayninger joked with me and told me a story about a husband who ordered his wife not to fast. He argued with her, and said: "I excuse you from the fast." At first his wife, who was a big eater, did not want to obey her husband. But soon she regretted her decision and kept asking her husband over and over: "Moyshe, what did you say to me before?" And her husband, playing stupid, answered her: "What are you talking about? I don't remember!" But she forced the issue: "What do you mean you do not remember what you said to me two hours ago?" "No," he persisted, "I really don't remember, it's escaped my mind." She continued to press him: "Moyshe, don't you remember something about not fasting?" And he shouted back: "Stop giving me a headache, I don't remember."

A story about poison for wild animals

Even though our honeymoon took place at the beginning of winter in my brother-in-law's village, we truly felt at home.

They had three children: two sons and daughter Rozya. His brother Sholem lived in an apartment next door. They were partners in managing the Rzhabtsh estate. Sholem's wife was called Pepi. She was around thirty years old. They had one son, a very charming boy, who was about ten. He was quite mischievous. One fine day while we were still in Rzhabtsh, he began to dig around in every corner. He saw a big hat box on top of the cupboard and took it down. Inside, he found big chocolate pastilles. He had a sweet tooth, and he shoved several pieces into his mouth in one fell swoop. At that precise moment, his mother came in and was horrified when she saw what he had eaten. She began to scream that he had poisoned himself. The hatbox contained poison pastilles intended for animals that they had often used when hunting. She flew over to her sister-in-law Yeti and looked up in the medical lexicon possible antidotes. A doctor was sent for. But before the doctor arrived, the little boy vomited everything up. When the doctor came to prescribe something for him, everything was already back to normal.

A *"ferbl"* with the young couple

We sat down to a home-cooked dinner of fried potato pancakes, gourmet coffee with heavy cream, and baked blintzes. After dinner, everyone—even your father—sat down to play *"ferbl,"* a type of card game. When your father's losses amounted to five Rheinisch, he stopped playing, and I was encouraged to take his place. Too embarrassed to refuse, I joined the game. I won back the amount he had lost, and then some. They did not understand me and certainly did not trust my intentions, because I seemed to play without serious interest.

Pepi, the red-headed card player

Pepi was exactly my opposite. While playing, she became even redder than she was normally. She had a white face, full of freckles, and fiery red hair. When she was angry, the white in her face together with her freckles became as red as her hair. She certainly played to win. Whenever she lost, Pepi became so agitated that it seemed as if she might attempt to kill herself.

Later, I asked your father to tell me a little bit more about her. He said that she had inherited her anger. Her grandfather Gedalie once tore a live rooster in half. In her family people were terrified to even mention his name because they had their suspicions about him. Apparently, he set out once with a partner to buy forest property but returned home without the partner. He could not sleep for an entire night. In the morning, a big white rooster appeared before his window and began to crow loudly. When Gedalie opened his window and leaped out, the rooster did not fly away but rather jumped up into his face. In fury he ripped apart the live rooster. Hence, the suspicion that he may have had something to do with his partner's disappearance.

The Levenherts family and their estate

When our relatives were invited to visit the Levenherts family in the nearby village of Pivavshtshizna they took us along with them. We went there one evening by sled. When we arrived they happened to be celebrating the birthday of Mrs. Levenherts. Mr. and Mrs. Levenherts were thrilled that we had come. Their oldest son, who was around sixteen years old, was even happier. They had three sons. All of them were successful. They had been taught well by an accomplished teacher. That night, after we had settled in, several other sleighs arrived with guests. The hosts ran out to greet them as excitedly as they had welcomed us. Whenever the dogs heard the bells of an approaching sleigh, they heralded the arrival of guests with their barking.

The first time in such aristocratic company

I must confess that this was the first time I was in such aristocratic company. The entire house looked regal. When we were led into the illuminated salon (though it was still without electricity), I thought that I was in the Garden of Eden. It was warm, bright, and you could see your reflection in the floors. They were bedecked with expensive carpets.

Well-dressed Ukrainians

The servants: several pretty, elegant Ukrainian girls wearing beautiful shirts embroidered in every color of the rainbow, corsets adorned with gold embroidery, and short, multi-pleated dresses like fans. They were covered in colored beads from their collars all the way down to their chests. Almost everyone's hair was chestnut, woven in two short braids, cut in layers, and plaited with all types of glittering beads. They wore their hair in cowlicks over their high foreheads. Throughout the entire house of about fifteen or sixteen brilliantly polished rooms, they hovered in white, felt slippers, like nymphs.

The younger Levenherts

As soon as all the guests had arrived, we were invited into the dining room. The Levenherts's eldest son—I do not remember his name—asked whether he could sit next to me at the table. On one side of me was your father, and on the other was this beautiful sixteen-year-old boy. Whether he sat to my left or to my right, I also don't recall. But

I do remember that we were both enchanted with one another; he because he was sitting next to a woman two or three years older (children always want to spend time with older company), and I, flattered that such an intelligent child was interested in me.

At the table

The table was tastefully set: beautiful napkins, lovely cutlery, and elegant dishes decorated with flowers. The food was prepared well, but not out of this world ... On the table, there were several vases with expensive, fresh flowers, most certainly from a greenhouse because it was already winter. At first, the table was set with fine torts and cakes. Then tea, coffee, and, if someone asked for it, chocolate. The young Levenherts, who was sitting next to me, put a lot of effort into entertaining me, and recounted several interesting anecdotes. He told me about the grand time spent with his teacher in Vienna, and how many interesting things he encountered there. He even met the children of the Kaiser's court in a Viennese park and endeared himself to them.

After bread and dinner (actually cake instead of bread), the company divided up according to age. The older men retired to the card room, the older women enjoyed themselves with gossip. We, the youngsters, went to the small salon where there was a stage and where a young woman, a neighbor of the Levenherts family, performed several comic sketches.

The family concert

We were soon summoned for supper. The meal consisted of two dishes: thick soup with pureed potatoes. But the potatoes were so specially prepared that they seemed more like a crispy knish. Of course, various meats were served. The toasts began during dessert. First, members of the family, then the teacher, who received a gold chain and watch with bold numerals as a gift. Later, the young Levenherts with the handsome black head of hair—he looked like an Apollo—declaimed something with great emotion and then sat down at the piano. He played a few pieces by Chopin, accompanied by the singing of his young neighbor from the village. The beautiful, deep music cast a spell over me.

When I got up from the table I no longer knew whether I was in this world or in the Garden of Eden. It was already late and all the guests were preparing to return home. My "admirer" helped me with my fur cape and gave me a beautiful bouquet of roses as a memento. He asked me to cover the box holding the bouquet with my coat so that his gift would arrive home with me in one piece. We sat down in the sleigh and sailed toward Rzhabtsh.

Rozya

Two days later, my brother-in-law Motl Hitner, his three children, your father, and I traveled back to Belz in a covered carriage because it was raining. My brother-in-law went to a barber shop and we waited with the children. Rozya, Motl Hitner's only daughter, was as beautiful as a rose. Motl was the oldest son of Grandfather Hitner. Along with Motl, there had been twelve sons. Even when Hitner's first wife died and he remarried, his second wife also bore him a son. As the only daughter in the entire Hitner family, Rozya received expensive gifts from her grandfather.

Rozya had chestnut hair, a white face, blue eyes, long black eyelashes, and a narrow white nose that almost looked as if it had been carved. Her chestnut hair stood out against the background of her elongated, white-rosy face with its slender red lips and brilliant white teeth. She was then about ten years old. On the other hand, Motl's son Buzye resembled his father. He had red, curly hair and a face full of freckles. The second son, Shunie, looked like Rozya.

Belz and the rebbe's court

While my brother-in-law was at the barber, his children guided us around the city. For me, it was nothing new: houses with big porches, grubby women sitting at stalls, many Jews walking around in fur hats and thin sheepskin coats, stained white shoes and stockings—all were certainly from among the *rebbe*'s followers. The children also showed us to the *rebbe*'s prayer house.

A tale with whiskers

We returned to the barber where the carriage was waiting for us. Rozya went into the barbershop to call for her father. Suddenly, we heard hearty laughter emanating from there. We followed her in and were greeted by the following scene: my brother-in-law was sitting in the barber's chair. His red beard was already shaved, but his mustache looked like that of a Polish Hussar. It stood out maybe five centimeters high and was twisted as thin as a needle. My brother-in-law's habit was to lose himself deep in thought and he had not been looking at himself in the mirror. Since he trusted the barber whom he had known for quite some time, he did not pay attention to how his whiskers were being trimmed. But when his daughter Rozya entered and took a good look at her father, she burst out laughing. She woke her father from his daydreams. When he caught sight of himself in the mirror, he too broke into spasms of laughter. When the owner of the barber shop heard the noise and loud laughter, he came in and apologized, explaining that he had been called out on an urgent matter and had left behind an apprentice in the middle of it all to substitute for him, but the new apprentice did not yet know his customers. The owner cut his red mustache, compared both sides of it to make sure it was even, and everything turned out fine in the end … I do not really know whether my brother-in-law is a daydreamer by nature or whether he was pretending he did not notice what was going on just so as to have material with which he could later entertain the village.

At the Yiddish theater in Lemberg

From Rzhabtsh, we traveled to Lemberg to receive our dowry and, at the same time, to attend the Yiddish theater. At the time, they were performing Goldfaden's *Lo takhmoyd* (Thou Shalt Not Covet). We were also at a performance of *Och, mężczyni, mężczyzni* (Oh, Men, Men) at the Polish theater. As a newly married woman, I saw in the Yiddish play an example of how one side can deceive the other in a match. And from the Polish performance, I learned that men can be false. I did not understand then that women know that trick even better than men, although things were not like that with me.

Returning from the honeymoon

When we returned home from our honeymoon with our relatives, the Hitners, an apartment was already arranged for us. Indeed, we arrived at night, and we were able to go straight into our own home. And because we were still being supported with board through the custom of *kest,* early the next morning we went to my parents for breakfast. I still remember how my father was sitting with my sister Laytshe at a big table loaded with books and doing the bills.

My father's bookkeeping

The daily journal was lying on the table. It consisted of several long sheets of white paper stitched together. Income and expenses were jotted down in this journal, which was always sitting on the big desk in the alcove: "one gone," "two gone," or "ten gone"—that was how mother noted her expenses for maintenance of the home and family. Business expenses and earnings were more precisely recorded. Every few weeks, father would sit down with Laytshe and enter everything in the main accounting book. When more had been earned than was usual, they would add "*mazltov*" in the columns. And sometimes my father would add the word "accurate" beside a big account. That is how he could be sure that he had not made an error.

(Another version of the previous three fragments)

Lemberg

On our way home to Redim from Rzhabtsh, we passed through Lemberg because we had brought documents with us that were necessary to collect our dowry, which was deposited in the mortgage bank there. We enjoyed ourselves in our free time. We spent two nights at the Bristol hotel. We attended performances of *Lo takhmoyd* at the Yiddish theater and of *Och, mężczyzni, mężczyzni* at the Polish theater. On the way back from the bank (it was already dusk) I remember how your father hid in a doorway. He was pretending to be a big city man, and he wanted to see whether I could find my way back to the hotel on my own. But I continued onward until your father came out from the doorway and caught up with me.

In our own nest

When we returned from our honeymoon to everyday life, our apartment was already arranged. It consisted of a small, tidy room with two steel beds, a table with four chairs, a small mirror and an oil-cloth sofa. With our own guests and a dowry of five thousand Gulden on top of it all, we already felt like real householders.

The first day of kest

But we still relied on eating our meals with my parents. Early the next morning, we went to my parents for breakfast. They did not live very far from our apartment. I still remember today how my father was sitting with my sister Laytshe at the big table by the window. It was still dark and a lamp was lit. The table was strewn with books. Father and Laytshe were sitting and doing the bills. Father shot an angry look our way and said: "Look who's here." He meant that while he was sitting laboring away, we were being pampered.

My father hated any help with the books, and Laytshe hated help even more than he did. She feared that Father would see that someone else could do it as well as she could. She did not allow anyone near the books and they remain with her to this very day. When she fled during the war, she took the ledgers with her. They are still in Pshemishl with the Gutt family. Perhaps the grandchildren—Laytshe's children—destroyed them.

My father's bookkeeping

While fleeing during the war, we left behind all the valuable silver—real antiques. But the account books with the debits that had not been collected were guarded like precious jewels. This is how the bookkeeping was done. There was a daily journal constructed of several sheets of narrow white paper, stitched together the length of the margin. In a corner, there was the inconspicuous notation "Receipts." Mother recorded all her expenses of the household in that book. I can visualize her big ones and twos: one-gone, two-gone ... and so on. The earnings and expenses from the grain, alcohol, or lumber trade were also jotted down along with the date and a short explanation. Business expenditures were always transferred immediately to the main account book. Every village had several pages for the debts of the peasants. The books were sealed with stamps. When a certain deal was particularly sweet, they added: "Purchased, with good fortune, ten acres of forest," and so on. When everything was transferred from the daily log book into the main account book, my father would count the earnings and mark down the word "accurate" in the journal. There was rarely an error. All this was done without an accountant, without double-entry bookkeeping, without "debits and credits," without the "American" system, yet it turned out all right.

Our first independent businesses

We ate our meals courtesy of my parents and slowly began to lend out our dowry. Father arranged a large book to keep track of our "credits and debits" and he taught me how to make proper entries in it. Without my knowledge, he had been lending money whenever possible to whomever needed it. He lent a small amount to his brother Zekharie and to Turnhayt, a pretty cousin from Yerslev. They left for Munich without returning the money they had borrowed. But from Munich, they sent a porcelain pitcher with the inscription: a memento from Munich. If that pitcher still exists, it is a collector's item.

Several years later, your father went into business with grandfather's money and with grandfather as a partner.

I forgot to tell you that for several years your father leased a distillery along with my brother-in-law, Avrom-Hirsh, who had already moved away from Mikhalovke and was living with his family in Redim. They fattened cows on the natural waste from the brewery and sold spirits to tavern keepers. Another time, your father leased a distillery in Kolnikov with my brother Neta. But, as I recall, he made no money from either business. We were supported by my parents. The rest of our needs such as our apartment, a wet-nurse, a maidservant, heat, light, and clothes had already devoured the remainder of our dowry. Your father bought the concession for marketing of spirits for the district from the Volfeld and Gotleib company of Ostrov with grandfather's money. But that business also left us destitute. This was because the times indicated—

(At this point the family memoirs abruptly end)

Hinde Bergner, Carlsbad 1913

Glossary

Abaye and Rava: prominent rabbinic authorities from the academy at Pumbe-
dita in Babylonia. The discussions and disputes of Abaye (278–338 C.E.)
and Rava (d. 352 C.E.) constitute a significant element of the Talmud.

benzkunim: the last child born to parents in their old age.

bris: circumcision ceremony.

"Daß der Rabbi und der Mönch": line from Heinrich Heine's poem "Disputation," which involves a debate between a rabbi and a Franciscan monk
over the fundamentals of faith.

Days of Awe (Heb. Yamim Nora'im): the period between the Jewish New Year
(Rosh Hashone) and the Day of Atonement (Yom Kippur).

dreydl: a four-sided top spun by children in games of chance during the holiday
of Hanukah. The four sides are inscribed with the Hebrew letters *nun,
gimel, heh, shin*, the first letters of the expression "*Nes gadol haya sham*—
a great miracle happened there."

esrog (Heb. *etrog*): a type of citrus fruit; one of the four species used during the
synagogue service during the festival of Sukkot (Tabernacles), an autumn
holiday marking the Israelite wandering in the desert. Silver and carved-
wood boxes for the esrog are common pieces of Jewish ritual art.

fifteen fruits: the fifteen different kinds of fruit, especially those from the Land
of Israel, eaten on Tu B'shvat, the festival of the new year of trees.

Gehinom: The "Valley of Hinnom" near Jerusalem where children were once
sacrificed in the Moloch sacrifice. Due to its bloody connotations, Gehinom is used by Jews as the place where evil-doers will be punished after
death.

gemore: another name for the Talmud, a vast compendium of rabbinic discussions constituting the Oral Tradition.

goy: "nation"; reference (sometimes derogatory) to a non-Jew.

Hakhmas ha-yad: "Wisdom of the Hand"; palmistry drawn from Jewish mys-
ticism; likely refers to the book by Moses ben Elijah Galina (fifteenth century), published in Hebrew and Yiddish in Warsaw in 1882.

hallel: psalms of thanksgiving and joy (Ps 113–118) added to the liturgy during the three ancient pilgrimage festivals.

Hear O Israel (Heb. "Shema yisroel"): the first words of the fundamental
expression of Jewish monotheism (Deut 6:4).

Kadish (Heb. kaddish): prayer recited by mourners after the death of a close
family member.

kest: marriage arrangement providing food and lodging, usually financed by the bride's family.

Khanike (Heb. Hanukah): the festival of lights lasting eight days that commemorates the victory of Jewish forces under Judah Maccabee and the re-purification of the Temple in Jerusalem around 164 B.C.E.

kheyder (Heb. heder): the traditional school where Jewish children first learned Hebrew, prayers, and Bible. These rudimentary schools were often located in a room in the teacher's house.

khosid, pl. *khsidim* (Heb. Hasid, Hasidim): "pious one"; a follower of the religious revivalist movement known as Hasidism, founded in the latter half of the eighteenth century by Israel Ba'al Shem Tov and his followers. By the mid-nineteenth century, Hasidism was the dominant form of Jewish religious identification in Eastern Europe, outside of Lithuania. Among other things, it was marked by charismatic leadership, ecstasy in prayer, group cohesion, and a popularization of elements from the mystical tradition.

kidesh (Heb. kiddush): "sanctification"; the ceremonial blessing recited over a glass of wine on Sabbath, festivals, and other joyful occasions.

Kidushn: "betrothal"; Hinde is referring here to the fact that guests keep drinking a kidesh to sanctify and toast her marriage.

Korbn-minkhe: title of a Yiddish prayer book especially popular among women.

kvater, kvaterin: ceremonial godparent; the individual(s) honored with carrying the baby boy to the person who holds it during circumcision.

Leyb Landoy: Jewish lawyer who became famous defending a Jewish student falsely charged with an assassination attempt on the Polish president in 1924.

Lo takhmoyd: "Thou Shalt Not Covet"; alternate title of Yiddish playwright Abraham Goldfaden's drama *Dos tsente gebot*, which premiered in Lemberg in 1894–95.

Mayse bukh: "Book of Stories"; vast, anonymous Yiddish collection of stories, folktales, legends, and oral traditions culled from talmudic and medieval Jewish lore. First published in 1602, it remained one of the most popular Yiddish books, especially among women, into the twentieth century.

maskil: adherent of the haskole (Jewish Enlightenment).

mazltov: "good luck"; congratulations.

melamed: traditional primary school (kheyder) teacher.

mezuze: "doorpost"; the parchment scroll with Torah verses from Deuteronomy 6:4–9 and 11:13–21, which is placed in a container and affixed to doorposts of Jewish homes. In Ashkenazic folk belief, the mezuze is often supposed to ward off evil spirits. If misfortune befalls a particular household or community, the parchment in the mezuze would be checked to ensure that it was still ritually unblemished.

peyes: side locks of hair beginning at the temples, which may not be shaven.

pidyen: "redemption"; in hasidic practice, a small payment provided to the rebbe in return for his blessing or intervention.

pidyen haben: "Redemption of the first-born"; according to biblical injunction, every first-born of the womb is considered to belong to God. The ceremony of redemption of the first-born occurs on the thirtieth day after the birth by paying a sum to a member of the priestly class, and is accompanied by the recitation of special blessings.

Rashi: Rabbi Solomon Itskhak ben Isaac (1040–1105); one of the greatest biblical and talmudic commentators of the medieval period.

Reb: honorific title of address (similar to the English "Mister").

Rebbe: charismatic Hasidic leader, sometimes referred to as a tsadik, who is seen by his followers to be a direct intermediary with God.

Rebetsin: the wife of a rabbi; also used here by children for the wife of a teacher.

serwantke: glazed-glass cabinet.

Shabes: Sabbath.

shadkhn: matchmaker or marriage broker.

shaytl: wig worn by traditional Jewish women after marriage as a form of modesty.

sheygets: a Gentile boy or young man; also used derisively to refer to young Jewish males whose behavior is deemed un-Jewish.

shidekh, pl. *shidukhim*: marriage matches, traditionally arranged between parents with the assistance of a matchmaker.

shtetl: a Jewish market town in Eastern Europe.

shtrayml: fur-edged hat worn by Hasidic Jews for the Sabbath and other festivals.

Shvues (Heb. Shavuot): "Weeks"; one of the three ancient pilgrimage festivals to Jerusalem, originally celebrating the spring harvest and the offering of the first fruits; now marked as the festival commemorating the giving of the Torah at Sinai.

szlaban: toll booth in the middle of roads at which all travelers had to stop a pay a duty on the construction of new roads. Jews were leased the duty of toll collection from the government.

tales-kotn: also known as "arba kanfes" [the four corners]; rectangular garment with knotted fringes on each of its four corners worn by observant Jewish males underneath their daily clothing.

Talmud: vast canonical text containing the discussions, deliberations, and legal opinions (halakhah) of post-biblical rabbis. There are two Talmuds: one produced in Babylon (the Bavli) and the other in the Land of Israel (the Yerushalmi). The Talmud remains the central text of Jewish scholarship and study.

Tenth of Tevet: a public fast that falls in winter commemorating the siege of Jerusalem.

Hinde Bergner

Tsena-urene: "Go forth and see [ye daughters of Jerusalem]" (Song of Songs 3:11); Yiddish version of the Torah that includes rabbinic commentaries and legends, especially popular among women.

tsitis: knotted fringes that all males must wear as commanded in the Bible in Numbers 15:37–39.

Tu B'shvat: holiday celebrating the new year for trees.

Wiener Israelit: German-Jewish newspaper from Vienna, published in the Hebrew alphabet, issued between 1862 and 1896, with significant gaps in publication.

yarmulke: skullcap worn by observant Jewish men and boys as a sign of piety and humility before God.

yikhud: "union" or "joining"; period of time spent alone by a bride and groom after the wedding ceremony. The bride and groom may eat a meal during that time together to consummate the marriage symbolically.

From Hinde Bergner's handwritten manuscript

122